The Seven Myths of Selling Your Home

with

20 Secrets You Need To Know

by

Chuck Marunde, J.D.

The Seven Myths of Selling Your Home, with 20 Secrets You
Need to Know
First Edition, March, 2015
Copyright 2015 by Chuck Marunde

Printed in the United States of America.
Publisher: Sakal Publishing
Chief Editor: Sabrina Marunde

Chuck Marunde may be contacted by email at
chuckmarunde@gmail.com

Cover Photo by Chuck Marunde

The Seven Myths of Selling Your Home, with 20 Secrets You
Need to Know
ISBN: 978-098-988-6338

Table of Contents

Other Books by Chuck Marunde

Buying & Selling Real Estate in the Rain Shadow
(Paperback, Kindle, and iPad)

Sequim Real Estate: A Buyer's Guide
(Paperback)

Buying & Selling Real Estate (Kindle)

Buying Your Retirement Home (iPad)

How to Make an Offer (iPad)

The New World of Marketing for Real Estate Agents
(Paperback)

The War for America's Soul (Paperback)

Success & Eternity (Paperback & Kindle)

About the Author

Chuck grew up in Alaska in a 900 square foot cabin with his parents, two sisters and two brothers. Their cabin was heated with a 55-gallon barrel welded into a wood stove, and it took 10 cords of wood to keep the cabin warm every winter. A single kerosene lantern hanging from a 16-penny nail lit the entire cabin. Temperatures in the deep interior of the state often dropped to 70°F below zero. A trip to the outhouse was a lonely trek in the middle of a dark winter night.

Life in remote Alaska was harsh in the '60s and '70s, but it was also rich with experiences and valuable lessons for life. At an early age Chuck's father taught him how to fend for himself and how to survive in one of the harshest climates in the world.

After graduating from the University of Alaska with a B.A. in Economics, Chuck got his teaching credentials and taught high school for two years. He then married and started a family while attending

Gonzaga University School of Law in Spokane.

Chuck joined the USAF and served four years as a Captain and JAG. After the military, he worked for Chuck Colson and Prison Fellowship Ministries as Area Director of Nevada and Utah. He was drawn back to Washington as he looked for a safe place to raise his children. That's when he found Sequim, Washington, and finished 20 years of law practice in Sequim.

Chuck is a real estate broker in Sequim, Washington with one of the largest Internet marketing systems in the Northwest. He is the author of thousands of online real estate articles and several real estate books in paperback and ebook versions. He does his own writing, editing, graphics, and publishing. He designs and builds all his websites and blogs and does his own SEO (search engine optimization). His real estate blogs are read by millions of people.

Chuck is a consistent top producer and was the number one individual selling agent of single family homes in Clallam County, Washington in sales volume in 2013. He was recognized for outstanding customer service among 25,000 real estate agents in Washington State, which includes the Seattle-Tacoma metropolis, receiving the prestigious *Five Star Real Estate Award for 2014*. He was featured in *Seattle Maga-*

zine in the December 2014 issue.

But here's the best part saved for last.

Chuck's proudest legacy would be his four children. Chuck's oldest son, Jesse, became a professional strongman, and the second strongest man in the world in Chengdu, China. He became famous around the world and especially in Europe where the Strongman contests are more popular. He had a heart to help young kids and changed a lot of lives for the better. But as many of Chuck's older clients would testify, life doesn't always go according to plan. Jesse had a heart attack while working out in his Sequim gym. He was gone at 27. That was eight years ago. Only two weeks earlier the family shared the joy of Jesse's first daughter being born. Chuck is often introduced as Jesse Marunde's father, a title he proudly wears.

Chuck's second son, Bristol, is also a professional athlete as a mixed martial artist living in the fight capital of the country, Las Vegas. In addition, he is a fight promoter, a real estate investor, and has his own wonderful family with two of the cutest boys on the planet. When Chuck is introduced to anyone in the mixed martial arts world, he is introduced as Bristol Marunde's father, and proud of it.

Brady is the basketball player and commercial

fisherman of the family. At 6'4" he is quite an athlete, too. He is also a generous and gifted young man. He lives in Las Vegas in the winters and is a commercial fisherman in Alaska during the fishing season. Around Sequim for years Chuck was regularly introduced, and still is, as Brady's dad. More proud moments.

And Sabrina is Chuck's daughter. She is now a college freshman. Her senior performance as Maria in the Sequim High School play, *The Sound of Music*, surprised a lot of Sequim residents with her natural acting and musical gifts. The theater was packed with standing ovations every night. Around Sequim, Chuck is now being introduced as "Sabrina's dad." How could a father be prouder?

How does Chuck describe his life now? "I have an incredible life in Sequim. I love how all the pieces to the puzzle of my life fit together so perfectly right now, and I feel very blessed, because in my real estate business buyers trust me with the privilege of helping them find that ideal home where they will feel physically, emotionally, psychologically, and spiritually happy for the rest of their lives. And sellers trust me with the most important investment of their lives--their homes. What a responsibility, and what a privilege it is to serve the incredible clients I keep getting. I love what I do, and I love my life in Sequim."

Chuck's blog can be found at:

SequimRealEstateNews.com

Chuck's email is ChuckMarunde@gmail.com.

Quotes

"Chuck was the Realtor we called to sell our home. His views on how to list and market a home were right on point. He is amazing. He sold our home, and it wouldn't have happened without Chuck's knowledge, integrity, experience and thoughtfulness." Rick and Marilyn

"I've had the pleasure of working with Chuck to sell my parent's estate. It was a tough time to sell during the housing recession, but Chuck always kept things on the positive side. With his real estate law background, he offers sound, practical advice. I was always impressed with his company's tech savvy communications and Internet presence: weekly email updates, blogs, videos, links, Linked-in networking, etc. He is truly pioneering the future of buying & selling real estate." Brian M.

"We found a Realtor who knew not only how to list a property, but most importantly, he knew how to sell a property. Chuck is very skilled in current technology and uses that skill to advertise your property nationally. We were very pleased with Chuck, his honesty and integrity." Jerry and Teva

"My wife and I bought and sold two houses through Chuck. Chuck is first and foremost just a good person, and he carries his personal honesty and integrity over into his profession. He has the greatest depth of experience in real estate of any agent or broker I have known. I am impressed by the way Chuck has integrated Internet services into his real estate business. He probably knows more about this process than any other Realtor in the country." Steve L.

Read more testimonials in the Appendix.

Preface

I wrote this book with the idea that many home sellers need good, relevant, and honest information before listing and selling their homes. With that in mind, I share things I've learned in the real estate business going back almost four decades. Many of the tidbits I share I call "secrets" because so few home sellers know them. But there's another big reason I wrote this book.

There are a thousand traps for the unwary, and I don't want you to get caught in any of them. I hope that the honest and transparent approach I have taken in this book is helpful. By that I mean I hope it saves you time and stress, and I hope it helps you sell your home in the least amount of time and get the highest price possible.

It would be nice if a book like this could just be full of warm fuzzies and make everyone think happy thoughts about all things real estate. But you can't reveal secrets that harm home sellers without sharing the truth by pulling back the curtains.

I've always thought that a big part of success in this life is avoiding major mistakes. That was true during my tour in the military, and it was true during my 20 years as a lawyer. But it's also true in real estate. Success in selling your home certainly means avoiding major mistakes. Some of those mistakes that so many home sellers regularly make are explained by the seven myths I address. Just avoiding these mistakes could change your entire selling process.

If you avoid big mistakes and succeed in selling your home in the least amount of time for the most money possible, you will find yourself less stressed and much happier. So this book does seek to help you think happy thoughts, but first we must walk through the Valley of Myths. On the far side of the Valley you will find what you seek.

Introduction

It doesn't seem that long ago when we were still dialing numbers on a rotary phone. Remember that? And it wasn't very long ago when fax machines first became popular, and then cell phones, and computers, and the Internet.

When I was in law school at Gonzaga University in the early 1980s, John Stockton was playing college ball in the campus gym, and no one had ever heard of Bill Gates. In 1985 Larry Page, co-founder of Google, was 12 years old, Steve Chen, co-founder of Youtube, was 7 years old, and Mark Zuckerberg of Facebook was only one. Now they are all billionaires. Google is old among technology companies today, and even Google was only founded in 1998.

Now people all over the world are using the Internet and smartphone apps as though they've been around forever. We have online services of every kind and software in the clouds. We have social media used by billions of people, and we can communicate instantly with friends all over the world. For the first time in the history of mankind, time and distance have been rendered irrelevant.

We have seen advances in the past 10 years that most of us would never have anticipated. As the saying goes, "The only constant is change itself." But what we've been witnessing is not only change as a constant, but the acceleration of change. The real estate industry has been right in the middle of these extraordinary developments.

This book focuses on a very narrow aspect of all these changes—selling your home today. I will drill down to the most relevant changes that affect you as a home seller. Because many of these changes have snuck up on us, most people are still thinking like they did 20 years ago with respect to advertising and selling a home. But the world has changed. Buyers have changed. It's time for home sellers to catch up to *The New World of Marketing*.[1] That's what this book is all about.

Much of what has been said about how to sell a home today is clothed in myths. Sometimes I hear home sellers repeat these myths, and I wince politely. The challenge is that myths are hard to recognize. Selling a home is not a process you can put in a laboratory to define the exact formula for success.

It is possible to do everything wrong and still sell

your home, if you get lucky. But selling your home should not be about luck. It should be about implementing the most effective strategies to reach the most qualified buyers. Even if you do everything right, there is no guarantee you will sell your home quickly for the price you want.

It's interesting how myths get started. Rumors that are repeated enough often become "facts," and information passed on from person to person can get lost in the translation. To make matters more interesting, even with honest and intelligent people, things can get a bit complicated, because what you knew to be true about selling real estate in the last decade is almost certainly not true in this decade. So even if you used to be right, you may be wrong now.

The Merriam Webster Dictionary defines a myth as, "an idea or story that is believed by many people but that is not true." We all know myths abound in science, history, and religion, but I can tell you that myths abound in real estate, too, especially for home sellers today. And these myths trap home sellers into making bad decisions. If you, as a home seller, are going to make wise decisions, they must be fully informed decisions, and that means getting past myths to get the whole truth. Making important decisions with partial truths can have devastating outcomes.

If you decide to try a new restaurant, and it turns out to be a bad decision, it's not a big deal. You may have wasted $20.00. But when it comes to selling your home, you could lose tens of thousands of dollars with a bad decision.

And you could lose a year or two of precious time. *At the age of 65 or 70 what price would you put on a year of your life? What value would you put on a one year delay of precious plans to live somewhere else, perhaps closer to the grandkids?* If you are fully informed about what it takes to sell your home, you can make wise decisions, get your home sold as soon as practical, and net the most money possible from the sale of your home. But you've got to be able to separate myth from fact. This book will help you do that.

There's so much to know and learn about selling a home in today's market. Several years ago I wrote a book specifically for real estate agents entitled *The New World of Marketing for Real Estate Agents.* In that book I made my best arguments to my colleagues in the real estate industry that we need to adapt our business models to meet consumers where they are, and to better market our listings to the most qualified buyers using the most powerful marketing tools.

I was not bashful about being critical of old fashioned and outdated practices, but I was writing directly to my fellow Realtors® around the country. That book received some high praise, including a strong endorsement from a well known national real estate instructor and motivational speaker, Tom Hopkins.

For Home Sellers Only

This book is written directly to home owners who want to sell their homes now or in the near future. So the focus of this book is to help home owners think through the issues that are most important when it comes to selling a home, issues like marketing and advertising, reaching qualified buyers, negotiating, handling the due diligence issues, and hiring a real estate agent.

I spend a lot of time on what you need to know when it comes to hiring a listing agent. This is important, because I have learned that the vast majority of home sellers do not know what to look for in a listing agent. Few have developed a good interview checklist, so I have done the hard work for you and included one in this book. You should not be looking for the perfect Realtor, because there's no such person. But you definitely want to find a really good one, and there is an intelligent way to go about that. I've included my 26-Point Interview Checklist to help you formulate the questions and concerns you can discuss with the agents you interview for that job.

Traps for the Unwary

There are many traps for the unwary home-owner who wants to sell his home, and traps are usually hidden or disguised, which means they catch many people by surprise. I've spent a lifetime helping clients avoid these traps, and it's been quite an education. Thousands of home sellers get caught by traps that they could have avoided if only they had known. Why isn't all of this well known and publicized? The answer will not surprise you.

People who get burned in real estate or who had a bad experience with a real estate agent don't like to spend money to hire an attorney, and they rarely file written complaints with regulatory agencies or associations. In addition, newspapers have no stomach for investigating and reporting problems in the real estate profession, because a major source of their revenue is from brokers. The result is that home sellers like you never hear about all the people who have experienced nightmares.

The answer for the vast majority of home sellers who have been caught by a trap for the unwary is not to pour a lot of energy and money down a black hole with no resolution. Holding someone accountable for bad advice is almost always a dead end in real estate transactions, and we all know the justice system is broken.

In addition, people who have had a bad experience often feel guilty about their part in the decisions that were made, and they experience a combination of emotions, including frustration, anger, guilt, and remorse. Instead of sharing their experience to educate others and help them avoid the same nightmare, they decide to quietly move on with their own lives. This is not a criticism. The truth is, it is probably healthier to move on and not dwell on the negative experience.

Save Yourself Time and Money and Stress

My point in sharing the story about trapping in Alaska and in real estate is that I have spent a lifetime in real estate as a broker and as a real estate attorney, and I've seen thousands of good people get caught in traps for the unwary. I've watched sellers make wise decisions, and I've watched sellers make disastrous decisions. In 37 years, I've seen all kinds of good and bad decisions, and I've seen far too many good people get caught in traps that end up hurting them financially or causing long delays in their plans.

And then there is the stress. What price can you put on unbearable stress? When I was practicing law, after one to two years of litigation with a trial at the end, clients would often tell me it wasn't primarily the $20,000 to $40,000 they spent on legal fees and costs that really bothered them. It was the tremendous stress that lasted so long and never let up until the end.

Save yourself from the costly and stressful lessons from the school of hard knocks, and simply take my lifetime of experience and use it for your own benefit. I've been helping clients avoid the traps, and teaching them to separate myth from fact for decades. I love what I do, and I'm passionate about helping people. This is what qualifies me to write so boldly about myths in real estate.

I've written thousands of articles and published them free for consumers so they can apply the lessons of many who have gone before them. I've written several real estate books, and I give them away to prospective clients to help them avoid the mistakes others have made.

In real estate sales, myths abound. It is in the lack of knowledge and experience that myths are born. I cannot tell you how many times I have heard myths repeated by well-meaning people concerning how to sell a home, how to advertise it, how to negotiate the price, how to handle due diligence issues, and so on. These myths are believed and repeated by very intelligent and successful people.

Spielberg Killed a Dinosaur

For centuries people thought the world was flat because they lacked knowledge of the whole truth. And more recently, a lot of people were angry with Steven Spielberg when they saw an old photo of him leaning against a dinosaur prop from the movie *Jurassic Park*. The prop appeared to be a dead dinosaur. Apparently many people sincerely thought Steven Spielberg had killed a dinosaur. I don't know what to say about that, except our public education system is sorely lacking. In real estate the myths are usually more subtle and far less dramatic. But that only makes them harder to recognize.

Even if the average person is not wrong about what they know in regard to marketing and selling a home today, their knowledge and experience is still very limited if they have not been a real estate professional for decades. It takes at least 10 years[2] as a full time professional to become an expert, and it really takes much longer to digest a large amount of knowledge and experience through several real estate cycles, and apply that experience consistently with wisdom.

An experienced professional will also gain the experience of thousands of his clients over the years. I should add that the number of years in the profession do not an expert make. One must be teachable and constantly learning in order to grow personally and professionally. One could be in the business for 20 or 30 years and still lack knowledge and wisdom.

Even a homeowner who has bought and sold a few homes is far from an expert. It is normal to gain a false sense of confidence after a few successes. Many homeowners do have a strong foundation of knowledge on some aspects of buying and selling. But even a room full of homeowners who have each mastered some aspect of selling real estate still may not put it all together in a comprehensive way.

Remember the legend of the blind men who described an elephant? The story is worth recalling here.

> Once upon a time, there lived six blind men in a village. One day the villagers told them, "Hey, there is an elephant in the village today." They had no idea what an elephant is. They decided to go and touch the elephant so they could figure out what an elephant is.
>
> "The elephant is a pillar," said the first man who touched a leg. "Oh, no! It is like a rope," said the second man who touched the tail. "Oh, no! It is like a thick branch of a tree," said the third man who touched the trunk of the elephant. "It is like a big hand fan" said the fourth man who touched the ear of the elephant. "It is like a huge wall," said the fifth man who touched the belly of the elephant. "It is like a solid pipe," said the sixth man who touched the tusk of the elephant.

If six homeowners watched the sales process of the same home from beginning to end, each of them would almost certainly tell a different story. Based on their individual knowledge and life experiences, they would focus on different aspects of the process, and they would emphasize different parts of that process as most important. Each one would probably walk away with a different lesson on selling homes, but even those beliefs would be limited by their abilities to accurately interpret events.

I've heard homeowners explain how they would advertise to qualified buyers, but then listened while they talked about advertising in all the wrong places. I've talked to other homeowners who knew exactly where they would advertise if they had the ability, and yet they did not have a clue when it comes to negotiating. I've talked to homeowners who knew precisely how much their home should be listed for, and others who insisted on listing for $100,000 more than it was worth.

I've talked to homeowners who knew how to compare real estate agents, and others who thought they did but clearly did not. I've worked with homeowners who did everything right, and others who sabotaged their own sale. Here's what's so fascinating, and one of the compelling reasons I wrote this book. All of these homeowners were equally convinced they were right. Every single one.

What is The Goal of Every Home Seller?

I can't reach every homeowner who thinks about selling their home, but I can help some who read this book, and I can help them achieve their goal.

What is the goal of every home seller? ***It is to sell their home for the highest possible price in the least amount of time***. Myths can hinder that process or even kill the chances of selling a home. But I've learned that there is one more unspoken goal of every home seller. It is to get their home sold ***with the least amount of stress***. No homeowner wants to experience nightmares and extreme stress, but many of the common myths can contribute to night-mare scenarios and stress.

The purpose of this book is to save you time and money and stress as you list and sell your home. I sincerely hope that my experience in real estate will help you make wise decisions that will enrich you as you move into the next exciting phase of your life. If you do find this book helpful, please email me at:

chuckmarunde@gmail.com and let me know.

---

[1] From the title of my book, *The New World of Marketing for Real Estate Agents*, published in 2010 by Sakal Publishing.

[2] In 2008 Malcolm Gladwell published his seminal book on what it takes to become an expert in any profession. His book, *Outlier*, concluded that it takes a minimum of 10,000 hours to become an expert. The rule applies across any profession.

Myth 1
Traditional Advertising is
All You Need

The world has changed since you sold your last home. Traditional advertising no longer sells homes effectively. Traditional advertising includes ads in print newspapers and print magazines, newspaper classifieds, radio, TV, billboards, mass mailings by snail mail, print flyers and brochures, trade shows and trade magazines (or home shows), open houses, and cold calling.

The problem with traditional advertising in real estate is that it no longer works like it did for decades. Unfortunately many home sellers (and their agents) across the U.S. are still thinking in terms of traditional advertising, but the vast majority of buyers moved away from these traditional media years ago.[1]

Effectively promoting your home today requires an understanding of how buyers have changed their habits, how they think, what they want and what they don't want, where they search and how they search. Buyers do not search for homes today the way they used to, and that changes everything about where and how we advertise to them.

Once you really understand buyers, you must master how to reach them and communicate with them. You cannot just shove information down buyers' throats. That doesn't work. It's all about permission marketing, good and relevant information, the kind they actually want and need, and it's about giving them the precise information they need when they need it, and doing it in such a way that you connect with them emotionally. Marketing today has risen to entirely new levels, and buyers have been telling us exactly how they want to be treated and how to communicate with them, if we will only listen.

Interruption Marketing

Traditional marketing has been called "interruption marketing" by one marketing genius, Seth Godin. He coined that phrase in his book, *Permission Marketing*. What he meant by the term was that TV commercials and newspaper and magazine articles interrupt what you want to watch or read, and they shove unwanted sales pitches in your face. Telemarketing phone calls are of the same nature. They interrupt what we want to be doing.

Much of traditional advertising interrupts us when we least want to be interrupted. In the middle of a good movie you are watching with your loved ones you get interrupted by a commercial sponsored by a pharmaceutical company that openly talks about the most intimate sexual matters. If you're in a mixed group of people or younger kids, some of these commercials can be quite embarrassing. These types of commercials are the ultimate example of interruption marketing.

Are You a Fish?

Traditional advertising treats people like fish who have to be hooked and reeled in. This is the nature of traditional advertising, and most of us are more than delighted that we now have other options to research and buy products and services. Technology and the Internet have changed everything about how consumers shop, and they have changed everything about how homes are effectively marketed today.

How do I know these things? My finger is on the pulse of buyers seven days a week from morning 'till night, and I listen and watch like a hawk to understand exactly what buyers want and how they want it. I've worked with thousands of clients going back 37 years, and I asked my clients what they do and how they do it.

I communicate daily with buyers from all over the United States, answer their questions via email, blogs, social media, forums, text messaging, and on the phone. I hear their questions and their concerns. I talk to them about how they search for their real estate, what sources of information they find useful and credible, what sites they visit, and I find out what they love and what they avoid like the plague.

I also talk to real estate brokers around the country, because they call me for guidance. Many of them have read my book, *The New World of Marketing for Real Estate Agents*. They tell me what their frustrations are in advertising their listings. They tell me what works and doesn't work in their part of the country, and they tell me the weaknesses of the franchise brokerages where they work.

But I also work with over a hundred prospective buyers each year, and sell dozens of homes to buyers in my market. I ask these buyers questions about how they search for real estate, for their agent, and how they make their decisions. The information buyers give me is worth a fortune in marketing research.

Digital Metrics

I have been measuring what works and what doesn't work for decades, and technology gives us the power of accurate digital metrics to measure each advertising method. Traditional advertising doesn't do this. Traditional advertising (like print newspapers) just keeps throwing out hooks, trying to catch anyone who gets within range.

Compared to the accurate systems we have available today via technologies on the Internet for target marketing and measuring statistical results, print newspapers are like going back to the days of fishing in the Mediterranean 2,000 years ago.

Back then fishermen sailed to an area where they hoped they would find fish, they threw a hook or net overboard, and they waited. Today commercial fishermen have diesel powered boats with electricity, galley kitchens, and comfortable cots. They have electronic devices that measure depth, show the precise contour of the ocean bottom, and even outline fish on their monitor. They have accurate GPS that identifies their position within 10 feet, and they can monitor live weather reports.

What a difference 2,000 years has made in the fishing industry. In the area of marketing and technology, the last 20 years has been like 2,000 years in the fishing business. Advances in technology in the past two decades is mind blowing, and has changed all the rules of advertising real estate.

Today buyers vociferously object to being treated like fish that need to be hooked by a slick salesman. They want to be in control of their own destiny, and they don't buy real estate without careful research. They research, compare quality and prices, and they make careful decisions. Technology has given them that power, and they love it. In fact, it has dramatically and permanently changed their buying habits.

Buyers also want to be treated with respect. Effective and respectful marketing on the Internet is more than just lead generation and cold numbers. Most marketers miss this, but advertising a home for sale is all about building relationships with qualified buyers.

While many salesmen of yesteryear were very good with customer service using traditional methods, modern technologies have changed many of the processes that appeal most to buyers. CRM, or customer relationship management, is not what it used to be.

The Best of Traditional Advertising

Let's take a look at what traditional advertising in the real estate business has been for decades. You may already know this, but most of these traditional methods are no longer favored by buyers, and remember, buyers determine the rules. Not all traditional advertising methods are dead today, but many are certainly on life support.

Historically in the real estate business, advertising listings included several traditional approaches. I'll touch on six here.

First, running a listing in the Sunday print newspaper was at the top of the list, although that typically meant each listing would get rotated and would only be advertised once every 90 days. But every home seller expected to see their listing in the newspaper at least once.

Second, real estate magazines that were placed in magazine racks at restaurants, hotels and grocery stores became an important selling point in any listing presentation. But again, most listings were rotated, so a listing might only show up once in each advertising cycle. Real estate magazines became kind of a fad for agents, a place where they could show clients physical proof they were advertising their properties.

Third, personalized mass mailing (via snail mail) spawned an entire industry itself. Businesses cropped up selling names and addresses and even detailed demographic information. In the beginning, being able to personalize letters with "Dear John and Mary," was very impressive. I sent out thousands of those kinds of mail merge letters myself.

Today for a fee, an agent can find out the name of every member of your family, your phone number, your mailing address, the length of time you have lived there, your previous residences, your occupation, a very accurate estimate of your annual income, the value of your home, a list of all the magazines you subscribe to, and your social media postings. As with so many types of interruption advertising, all of this was carried too far.

Fourth, open houses became popular and a mainstay in traditional advertising. I held many open houses in my career, but only sold one as a result of the open house. That was in a very hot real estate market in Fairbanks, Alaska in the 1970s. Few agents ever sell a home at an open house.

Fifth, massive public advertising became a primary effort by large real estate franchises to capture customers. The popular term they liked to use was "branding." Huge billboards became all the rage. And they were expensive! Huge bricks-and-mortar buildings with large signage were also a sign of the times. Bigger was always better, or so they thought.

Sixth, expensive TV commercials (and radio) created competition among the big national brokerages. This was another effort to brand a name, so home sellers would automatically think of that company and list with them. Back then, all this worked. People didn't interview agents; they just hired them if they answered the phone and had a heartbeat. Thank

God clients are much more discerning today.

There were other lesser advertising techniques, but these were the major traditional advertising methods for listed properties. Let's take a closer look at five of these.

Print Newspapers

Print newspaper ads for real estate simply do not produce buyers anymore, especially in a rural area where most of the buyers are retirees coming from somewhere else in the country. I've been asking buyers for seven straight years if they subscribed to the local newspaper, and in all those years only two said they did. Even those two said the listings in the newspaper were very limited, so they used the online MLS to do a thorough search for their homes.

You might think that newspapers would be effective for advertising homes in metropolitan areas like Tacoma, Washington. They're not. People are using the Internet to search for homes. The newspaper probably includes far less than 1% of the MLS listings, and looking at the print classifieds doesn't allow buyers to search with their own unique parameters like they can online. This makes the print newspapers almost worthless for buyers.

Now you're probably thinking that the Sunday issue of every print newspaper is full of real estate listings. If print newspaper ads for real estate no longer sell real estate, why do agents keep running their listings in the print newspapers?

I wonder if you know the answer? I'll tell you, but pause for a moment to think about this, and let's see how close you are. Hint: It's not to find buyers for the homes they are advertising.

I called a colleague who advertised his listings regularly in the Sunday issue of a print newspaper. One weekend he spent about $300 running several of his listings, so I decided to have a little fun. The conversation went like this:

> <u>Chuck</u>. So tell me John [not his real name], I saw you had six of your listings in the Sunday newspaper. Did you sell some of those properties?
>
> <u>John</u>. A pregnant pause was followed by a drawling, "No."
>
> <u>Chuck</u>. Did you get some great leads?
>
> <u>John</u>. No, not really.
>
> <u>Chuck</u>. Did you get some good phone calls?
>
> <u>John</u>. I had one phone call. A tire kicker.
>
> <u>Chuck</u>. So John, why do you keep running your listings in the print newspaper when these ads don't sell real estate and when you don't even get good leads, and especially since it is so dog-gone expensive?

John. Well . . . (a pause punctuated by what I thought may have been a sigh) my clients expect me to advertise their properties.

Chuck. Right, but that doesn't answer my question John. If your clients asked you to jump off a bridge, you would politely decline. So why don't you explain to your clients what works and what doesn't work. Your clients are not going to want you to throw money over a bridge. Why not spend your advertising dollars on things that work?

John. Well, my clients want to see me advertising, and they expect to see their properties in the newspaper where other agents advertise, too.

Chuck. What they expect is that you will sell their property John. Trust me, they don't care about the rest.

John. Well, I've got to show them I'm doing something.

That's usually where we get on an endless loop with my friend repeating himself. No matter what else I ask or say, he just keeps repeating that mantra, "my clients expect to see their listing in the newspapers so they know that I'm doing something." I just shake my head.

I cannot over emphasize how deeply engrained this thinking is in agents' thinking. Even as I was editing this chapter, I got a call from a veteran real estate agent, and we happened upon this very subject. He immediately agreed with me that advertising listings in the newspaper was a waste of money, but he also said he does it because his clients expect to see their listings in the newspaper. This is an agent who understands, but still insists that he and his clients keep riding the traditional marketing Merry-Go-Round. Apparently he doesn't feel it is worth trying to educate his clients, or he thinks it would be a waste of time.

Then you get the agent who says, "Oh, no, advertising in the local newspaper works really well. I just sold a house I advertised in the paper. So there you go." One sale does not establish a rule. In fact, it only proves my point. If only one out of 1,000 homes sells as a direct and proximate cause of running a newspaper ad, for example, that would tell me newspaper ads are not effective.

There is usually much more to the story. Was that house that sold really a direct result of running the ad in the newspaper, or did that buyer find it on the Internet and it just happened to also be advertised in the newspaper? Or did the buyers have it saved on their favorites' MLS list for weeks or months before they came, and they would have looked at it anyway?

An agent without an understanding of how advertising works might sincerely believe that advertising one of her listings in the newspaper is a good idea and will help sell it. But if she was paying attention to nationwide advertising statistics on real estate and the metrics of her own print advertising, she would realize that print ads don't sell the homes advertised to the people who call on those ads. If someone calls off a newspaper ad, it is more likely they are just seeking information, and then they hang up. They don't like being sold on the phone anymore.

Even if they do agree to go out with that agent and look at homes, the odds are extremely high they buy a different home than the one they saw in the newspaper. This is a statistical reality all across the country.

While that scenario can work out for a listing agent, it does not accomplish the goal of selling the home advertised. It only gives that listing agent a lead who does <u>not</u> buy your home.

In support of their traditional advertising approach, agents are trained to rebut this with an argument relying on indirect causation. By advertising some listings in the newspaper, they are getting leads to sell other homes, homes not advertised in the newspaper. So their argument will be that even though it is extremely unlikely they will sell your home by running a print ad, nevertheless by running other clients' listings in the newspaper, they might indirectly sell your home. But the odds of selling any of the homes advertised in print is also extremely unlikely. The greater likelihood is that the agent will sell that buyer a home not in the newspaper, but in the MLS. The conclusion is that running listings in the print newspaper are for the benefit of the agents and not the home sellers of the ads.

The truth is print advertising is a form of branding for agents who hope that by adverting listings in the newspaper (that they do not sell because of the newspaper ad), that they will get more listings from people who see their ads and assume they are selling a lot of real estate. Do you see the irony of this? Let me say it a different way.

Listing agents who list, list, and list without also having a powerful marketing system to buyers, often advertise extensively in traditional media. They have to because they don't have a powerful online marketing system to buyers. So for example, by running their ads in the print newspaper, which does not sell the homes directly, they hope they will get more listings, so they can get more listings. That's not a typo in the last sentence. The goal is to get more listings, advertise them in the newspaper in order to get more listings, so other agents will keep selling those listings, so the listing agent can make money just by listing and not by selling herself. She gets lucky when she does sell one herself.

So an agent who is running a lot of traditional ads is able to tell his listing clients that he is really doing something. He is doing something. He's running expensive print ads, but that may be all he's doing. It's all about perception rather than reality. But the clients rarely figure any of this out.

Do you see why I say that print newspapers are not the best way to advertise your specific listing? I like to ask this question, "What is in my client's best interest?," not, "What is in my best interest?" What will help my client with no hidden agendas? I believe in transparent honesty.

Exaggerating One's Way to Success

There's one more irony that I cannot pass up. I know of agents in several markets who have exaggerated their way to success. One boasted of selling hundreds of homes until enough people believed him and listed with him assuming he was a Superman. Eventually he did sell a lot of homes because so many people listed with him. But it was a case of lying to hundreds and thousands of clients before enough of them took the cheese, and he got so many listings that other agents sold, that he ended up becoming a millionaire. Now people think he really is a great success. It may be success from his perspective, but I call it success without honor.

What happened to old fashioned honesty and integrity? I'll tell you. Consumers are not doing their homework and due diligence, and so lying pays off for many sales people without a moral compass.

Print Magazines

An interesting genre of magazine found a niche in the real estate industry about 25 years ago by selling real estate agents space to promote their listings. We generically called these real estate magazines, and usually they were about three dozen pages of solid listings. Agents could buy a quarter, half, or full page.

It was a stroke of genius for the magazine industry, because prior to this, magazines had to publish articles that they paid authors to write, and then they sold advertising space throughout the magazine to make money. These real estate magazines published no content, and only sold adverting. Not only did they not have to pay for content, they got paid for every page in the magazine. Talk about profitable! It was a gold mine for the magazine publishers.

But did these magazines sell real estate? That is still debated. One of the big limitations of print advertising is that there are almost no metrics to measure the effectiveness of expensive ads. There are only anecdotal stories by agents. When it comes to selling real estate, if you cannot definitively demonstrate that an advertising method works, it probably does not.

For a couple of decades these real estate magazines were a real money maker for the publishers, but then the world started changing. Advances in technology, the Internet, and changing consumer preferences disrupted traditional print advertising. The cost of doing business for real estate brokers continued to increase at the same time commissions were decreasing during recessionary times, and one of the biggest business expenses was print advertising.

Not only did agents stop buying $800 pages in the real estate magazines, consumers continued their shift away from print media to free online resources. So the real estate magazines got hit hard during the recession, and many went out of business.

These traditional print magazines are not an effective way to promote listings, but some agents are using magazines as part of their bigger strategy of "branding." The traditional notion was that if enough people kept seeing a business name over and over again, eventually when they need their service, they would just hire them. But buyers are much more discerning today.

I do know of one real estate magazine publisher who is trying to bridge the gap from the traditional print magazine to a new magazine concept that includes beautiful print magazines distributed only in high value locations along with an Internet mapping system. I am hopeful that this will be successful.

Open Houses

"Do open houses sell homes in small rural retirement communities?" The unequivocal honest answer is, "No!" We've known this for decades inside the real estate community. This doesn't mean you shouldn't have an open house, but if you do you should know exactly what agents know: <u>Open houses don't sell houses, but they do give agents new buyer leads</u>.

> *"I've done too many houses where no one comes, even the neighbors. And no one would have come even if I'd guaranteed the second coming of Jesus to occur," said broker William Metzker of Portland, Oregon-based Terradigm Real Estate Consultancy. "A few sellers want no part of them, but most do, because they've bought into the myth that people often buy homes during an open house," Metzker said. "Statistically, that's far from true."*

The purpose of an open house is first and foremost to promote the real estate agent. It's nice if you want to help your listing agent get new leads by letting him hold an open house, but don't be under the misconception that your agent will sell your home at the open house.

He or she could sell it, but the odds of that happening are probably less than 1 in 100 in a small rural market. There are better ways to spend time and money. As long as you understand that, you won't be disillusioned if nothing happens at your open house.

Accurate statistics on the success of open houses are sorely missing. What is clear is that on a nation-wide basis, open houses are a disaster as a marketing tool to sell a house at an open house. There are thou-sands of stories written by agents on the Internet affirming this. But there are nuances that account for different opinions on open houses. For example, met-ropolitan areas will have short spurts of success with open houses in extremely hot markets. In rural areas where buyers are largely retirees from other parts of the country, open houses are quite useless.

Less than 2% of homes sell at open houses in a normal real estate market according to the National Association of Realtors (NAR), and I'm sure that was in the metropolitan markets. In a real estate recession like the one we have experienced, my guess is that far less than 1% of homes sell at any open house weekend. And in a rural market where the buyers are almost entirely retirees from outside the area, proba-bly less than 1/10th of 1% of homes sell at an open house.

Redfin did a study of open houses, and they

concluded in part that, "In the other eight markets we examined, there was virtually no difference in the percentage of homes that sold, whether they had an open house or not. So should you hold an open house? If you're in San Francisco, absolutely. If you're in Phoenix or Las Vegas, probably not. Everywhere else, it most likely doesn't really matter whether or not you hold an open house . . ."

The Real Reason to Hold an Open House

So why would agents hold an open house in a rural area? There are two reasons. First, they hold open houses to satisfy their selling clients, to be able to tell them they are doing something to market their homes. I've heard agents say, "I've got to show my clients I'm doing something, anything."

The second reason is more substantive. <u>Agents hold an open house so they can get a list of prospective buyers</u>. There it is! The primary purpose of an open house is to generate leads for the agent.

Proof: Go to an open house and listen to the questions the hosting agent asks you. Do you live in the area? How soon do you plan to buy a home? Have you pre-qualified? What is your price range? What kind of work do you do? Do you both work? How many children do you have? Where do you live now? Do you rent or own? Would you sign-in here with your name, address, phone number, and email address? Why would you give an agent you have not even hired to represent you all this personal information?

Some astute buyers know that open houses can be a trap, and they actually avoid them rather than get into a conversation with an agent who is trying to hook them. Some buyers realize that the listing agent who is hosting the open house represents the seller, not the buyer. That listing agent has a legal and fiduciary duty to get the seller the highest possible price and the best possible terms. Smart buyers do not want to give the seller's agent all their personal information, information that could be used to negotiate against them.

Who actually shows up at open houses in a rural area? Curious neighbors, tire kickers, locals taking a Sunday drive and out for a little fun, **not** car loads of qualified buyers. Believe me, I've been there, done that too many times. Apart from the fact that open houses rarely sell a home, there are three reasons holding an open house for the public is not advisable.

<u>Open House Warning No. 1</u>: As a real estate broker, I periodically receive an email alert notifying me that there is a criminal frequenting open houses. That is a rare event in a small rural area, but it is not unheard of in the metropolitan areas. This alone might be a reason a homeowner, especially an elderly

couple, might choose not to hold an open house.

Open House Warning No. 2: Did you know that a homeowner who invites the public to attend an open house may be liable if one of those guests falls and suffers from an injury? We all know we are now living in a litigation prone generation, and it would be a tragedy if someone slipped and fell and then sued for a judgment equal to the equity in the home. Ridiculous lawsuits are far too prevalent in the U.S.

Open House Warning No. 3: This may be the ultimate reason a homeowner decides not to be involved with open houses. Open houses simply do not sell homes in rural areas, especially when the majority of buyers are from outside the area. They are a colossal waste of time and money.

Open Houses for Agents Only

There is one kind of open house that a home seller might consider, an open house for other real estate agents. It's nice to introduce other agents to a listing, but it's effectiveness is negligible, because if an agent has a buyer for a particular kind of home, he will show every available listing that fits those parameters.

The truth is agents haven't seen most of the listings in their market. A small MLS might have 800 listings. An active agent might have seen 10% of those listings. That means we show and sell listings that we haven't seen in advance all the time. A broker open house is near the bottom of effective selling techniques. It can't hurt, but it becomes a matter of where time and resources will be spent most effectively marketing a home. With the Internet, an agent can sit in his office and look at 50 homes and examine all the details and photos in the time it takes to drive out to look at one Realtor open house.

Now would you like to know why agents hold open houses for agents? Again, in a large metropolitan area the dynamics of open houses are different, and bringing agents could be helpful if one of those agents has a buyer for that exact kind of home and area.

But in a rural area, why would agents hold open houses for agents? It is rare that one of those agents would attend an agent open house and sell it as a result. The real reason for agent open houses in rural areas is to show the home seller that the listing agent is doing something to market the home. So agents do favors for each other by attending their agent open houses and leaving lots of business cards on the counters.

It looks impressive to a home seller. It seems like these people are really marketing up a storm. Again, this approach focuses more on appearances and perceptions than it does on effective marketing and advertising.

Now for any of these methods, there will always be someone somewhere in the United States who will say, "I sold a home that way," but one lucky sale does not prove the effectiveness of a method. In fact, it may actually prove the ineffectiveness if only a tiny percentage of sales out of a thousand sales are made using that method.

Billboards and Signage

Since most home buyers are using the Internet now, there are many old forms of advertising that have fallen to the wayside. Billboards were popular in the 1950s and the 1960s, and billboard companies still sold a lot of billboard space through the 1970s and 1980s, although their effectiveness was steadily declining. If you drove anywhere in the U.S. on major highways in the 1960s you couldn't help but see those cigarette billboards: Marlboro, Lucky, Winston, and Camel.

Today, you will still see some billboards along the highways, but they are mostly a source of advertising revenue for the large companies that own them, and few businesses waste their money on billboard advertising. They are not an effective way to advertise most businesses or professional services anymore, if they ever were.

I should point out that Las Vegas is on a different planet, so advertising with billboards in Vegas does not play by the rules of the rest of the galaxy. You won't see real estate brokerages advertising on billboards in Vegas, but you will see the big three—sex, enticements to great wealth, and personal injury attorneys.

It is a sign of the times to see empty billboard space that cannot be sold, and the familiar, "This Space Available." What a lot of billboard companies are doing now is leaving the last advertiser on the billboard, even though his contract expired and he's not paying anymore. At least that makes it appear that someone is buying billboard space when the truth may be no one wants it.

There is a new kind of billboard, which is the brightly lit and colorful electronic billboard. These are certainly more visible, but they are incredibly expensive to buy and put up, and therefore, very expensive to rent. You won't see many of these, and when you do it will be in a metropolitan area advertising a big car dealership or a casino. Car dealerships have suffered, and many have closed, but the biggest ones advertise like crazy. Casinos advertise a lot and do well in good and bad times, but Casinos have more money than God.

TV and Radio Commercials

Buyers from outside a local real estate market are not listening to local radio stations, yet traditional real estate advertising spends valuable dollars on radio ads. In the major metropolitan areas, large franchises plan their advertisements carefully for the entire year, and they will use radio and TV as part of their branding strategy just to imprint their name on people's minds.

In rural areas or in small towns, small business owners use radio as an experiment. They don't have the metrics or the hard data to help them make the best financial decisions when it comes to advertising, so they run ads on a local radio station, but in real estate sales, most agents give up on advertising that is no longer generating quality leads.

I'm one who is always tweaking my own marketing and the advertising I do for individual listings, and sometimes I go back to try something that has not been working. I experiment with my own money to try various methods, and I test and test and test.

So last year I was persuaded by a good man (and a friend) at a radio station that radio spots would generate business and solid leads for me. We talked over a period of weeks, educating each other to the changes in how buyers search for a retirement location and real estate and their agent. He's been in radio for a long time, and he's a sincere salesman, so I value his experience and opinion.

I started in real estate sales 37 years ago, practiced as a real estate attorney for 20 years, and authored several real estate books, including one entitled *The New World of Marketing for Real Estate Agents.* I've built the most successful virtual brokerage in my market, and agents from around the country often call me for help, so I'm considered an expert in real estate transactions and marketing. As I look back over the past 10 years, nearly all of my predictions about the real estate industry and the changes that would occur came true. So it was hard for me to write a check for traditional advertising that I had been accurately predicting for 10 years would be slowly dying.

The point is, we both had something to offer each other, and our conversations about marketing and how consumers engage real estate agents to buy and sell real estate were good conversations. I insisted that radio no longer was an effective medium to reach clients in the real estate business, and my friend heard me out but persuaded me that there was a demographic that did listen to radio who would respond and generate business for me. I was persuaded to sign an annual contract with two daily radio spots for a total of $7,000.

You've got to see the irony in this. Here I was, the preeminent virtual real estate broker on the Olympic Peninsula, one of the top selling agents of single family homes in the county, someone who has written extensively about the death of the traditional bricks and mortar brokerage, an analyst who wrote about the failure of traditional advertising to generate real estate leads, and I was signing a contract to advertise on a radio station, one of the oldest and most traditional forms of advertising.

Why would I do that? Because even when I am convinced that the evidence demonstrates a certain kind of advertising is not effective, I am still teachable. I could be right one year, and wrong the next year. The key to growing personally and professionally in my opinion, is being teachable and constantly observing and learning.

Any agent who is not adapting in this rapidly changing environment will eventually be out of business. The last agent home sellers need today is one who is still practicing what he or she was doing 10 or 20 years ago. Some of the big brokerages are leading from behind, and that's not working for a lot of clients today. I have always worked to be out in front where the action is, which is also where the buyers are showing up in large numbers.

So how did my radio advertising work out? Did

it generate a lot of business? Did it at least pay for itself? The answers are: not very good, no and no. I would have loved to say the salesman was right, that radio advertising for real estate really works. But it did not generate a single client. Not one. My friend was surprised, but I was not. I refrained from saying, "I told you so." But for $7,000 and no return on my investment, I think I would have been entitled to say, "I told you so."

As I reflect on this experience (and wasted advertising), I am realizing there was something very important I did not think about when my friend persuaded me to advertise on the radio. While I had many years of data that proved to me that radio was not an effective way to advertise real estate, my salesman friend did <u>not</u> give me a single example of any other broker like me who testified that spending money on the radio worked for them. I had heard some brokers advertise from time to time on the radio, but none of them stuck with it. That should have told me that my instincts were right.

I don't believe in guessing about what works or doesn't work. I find out with hard work and real money, then I examine the results objectively. That's what serious marketers do. If anyone wants to contradict any of the facts or opinions in this book, ask them what data and what facts they have to back up their statements. Make them prove to you that what I am writing in this book is objectively not true. They will not be able to do that. I have proven everything I do over and over again. If it doesn't work, I don't waste time or money on it. If it works exceedingly well, then for the sake of my clients, I will do more of it and perfect it. But if it is a colossal waste of time, I don't bother.

TV advertising is simply too expensive for individuals in real estate. The large franchises advertise on TV as part of their global branding effort. I wish someone would tell them that buyers are not paying any attention to those multi-million dollar commercials. Too often in the business world it's all about perception.

Berkshire Hathaway's real estate brokerage has a TV ad in which the only thing the agent says to her client is, "There are a lot of buyers for homes like yours." It's clear that with the music and the setting, you are supposed to feel like the agent just pronounced wisdom from on high, and the camera zooms in on the seller who looks like he just had the happiest thought in his life.

That's the substance of how a brokerage expects to persuade you to hire one of their agents? Do they really think consumers are so shallow?

Apparently.

I'm more interested in what works, and home sellers are starting to question traditional approaches. That's good, because as I will say more than once, "the answers you get are only as good as the questions you ask."

The Curse of the Bricks and Mortar

If anyone is entitled to criticize the real estate profession, it would be another full time real estate broker like me with a lifetime of experience. This is my profession, and I'm proud of what I do and how I do it, but I also know the business inside and out after 37 years, and that gives me the right to critique my own profession, especially because of my passion to protect consumers and to give them what they want and expect.

I was a real estate attorney for 20 years, and as a lawyer I was often critical about the justice system. It's no secret the justice system is broken, and I wasn't bashful about saying that, or sharing that lawyers did not always serve the best interests of their clients. I was right about the legal profession, and I'm right about the real estate profession.

But I'm also teachable. I listen and I learn every day. I learn what does work and what doesn't work, and I can testify that we are in an extraordinary time of change. It's both exciting and scary.

Reaching qualified buyers is everything today, and buyers have shifted their focus away from annoying interruption advertising, and they have moved to entirely new methods of communication. For the big offices, the phone isn't ringing off the wall anymore, and buyers don't waltz into bricks-and-mortar real estate offices anymore, at least in large numbers.

This doesn't mean a bricks-and-mortar office is not useful. An office is cool, but it can cost a fortune in overhead to own or lease, and buyers and sellers do not actually care about the office anymore. Of my last 100 clients, I believe 2 asked about the office, and they didn't feel the need to go to one. The other 98 never asked. If they needed to and wanted to meet in an office, then an office would be essential. It's not anymore. Why?

Sellers want their agents to come to their home. And that makes sense, since an agent must first see the home to evaluate it and to do a comparable market analysis. Even during the term of a listing, agents typically do their clients a service by going to the home for meetings. That is much better personal customer service than telling a client, "Come down to my office and wait in the front room for 30 minutes until I get to you."

I love irony, and here's some irony for you. I do have a small bricks-and-mortar office myself, but frankly my buyers love meeting at Starbucks before we head out to look at homes. This probably requires a brief explanation. The reason clients enjoy meeting with me at Starbucks and taking off after a hot Latte and some conversation is because we already have a relationship that we have been building for weeks and in most cases months.

My clients tell me they feel like they already know me, the way I think, the way I talk, the way I gesticulate having watched some of my videos, and having read many of my articles. Some have read one of my books. There is a sense of excitement when we meet and get ready to go out and look at the homes we've been discussing for months. You can see the obvious importance of building good relationships with buyers with this kind of marketing.

But if I was sitting in an office waiting for the phone to ring or waiting for a stranger to walk in the door, and if that's how I relied on generating leads to sell homes, I would be a bit desperate in this day and age. It would be a lonely assignment to have "desk duty" watching a phone that doesn't ring. The reality is those walk-ins are not buyers who have been doing their homework and know exactly what they want, and they are not normally ready to buy anything.

These are additional reasons that an office today does not have the same usefulness it did two decades ago.

My little office is unique among real estate offices. It is downtown, and it does not have any 600 pound Army surplus desks. In fact, it doesn't have any desks. It has a variety of comfortable chairs, sofas, and tables with what I would describe as a coffee shop environment, casual but classy. It's private, quiet, comfortable, and conducive to having enjoyable conversations, and for drafting contracts or doing presentations. There is an audio and video section for watching anything and doing presentations. There is classical music playing softly. There is a special coffee and tea maker, and a refrigerator full of fresh healthy drinks for clients. Everything is wireless, and while it looks simple and classy, this may be the most powerful office in the county in terms of real estate resources and expertise.

But this little bricks-and-mortar is not an advertising technique to buyers or sellers. No office today effectively generates leads, at least not enough to seriously call it an effective tool to sell homes. The office is a place to meet or teach people after you've already connected through other means. That's not the way it used to be, but it is today. Still I find it humorously ironic that the number one virtual broker in the Northwest has a bricks-and-mortar office. I love it.

The Hidden Agenda

There is one other powerful psychological function of a traditional office that I doubt most people are even aware of. The traditional office uses a number of classic client control techniques. Top salesmen are taught that to close a sale, they must control their client, which means there can only be one alpha in the room. To have that control from the beginning of a relationship, the traditional office uses a number of architectural features and psychological control mechanisms.

First, there is the lobby with a receptionist. When you walk in you are told to wait in the lobby until your salesman comes out, which sometimes is a long time. All of that has the affect of psychologically showing you who is in control, and it's not you.

Second, you will normally be taken into a conference room, and again the salesman is in control and the seating is arranged to make that clear. If an agent takes you into his office, sometimes you will see the old school technique of having you sit in a chair that is slightly below the salesman's chair, so again a subtle but continuing sales technique to make sure that you know your place.

These are long established and proven psychological methods to control a client in a subtle way without the client even realizing it. The whole idea is that when the salesman is in control and you are subservient, he can persuade you to sign the contract or close the deal.

My office has none of these control techniques. No lobby. No receptionist or gatekeeper. My office has very comfortable furniture, but my clients and I are seated equally. There is no alpha control system in place.

Why do I not use these long established psychological sales techniques? Because knowledge, competence, professionalism, and honesty trump all the gimmicks. Without a strong foundation in these things, in order for an agent to sell you, he might have to distract you with humor all the time, or change the subject when your questions are too hard. Then you need gimmicks, including every psychological sales trick in the book.

My clients get my respect, and I earn their respect. I serve their best interests from beginning to end, and if it is in my client's best interest not to write an offer, sign a contract, or to terminate a transaction, I do that without hesitation and regardless of any commission.

In other words, there is no need to control my clients. In my business model, I serve my clients' best interests, not mine. I don't need to be the alpha in control, but my clients also don't feel they need to control me. Maybe this is why my clients and I have such fantastic relationships.

Not only is the traditional office unnecessary now, but even traditional advertising falls far short of effectively promoting a listing today. In fact, much of traditional advertising is on life support today. The entire real estate business is changing, and we've only touched the tip of the iceberg.

Let's look at the next myth.

---

[1] Secret No. 1. Traditional advertising no longer works like it once did to sell homes, and that's a very polite way to say that traditional advertising is on life support. While many get this, most do not know the dramatic ways that an effective advertising matrix has changed.

Myth 2
You Need a Listing Agent to Sell Your Home

Let's clear up a major misconception about listing properties and listing agents. I believe a majority of home sellers are under the assumption that they should list their homes with a listing agent, who they believe specializes in marketing properties like theirs. Before we're done with this chapter, you'll see why this is a myth.

Most people tend to classify agents as either listing agents (sellers' agents) or buyer's agents. Twenty years ago this classification made sense, but the world of real estate has changed. You'll also see why this classification is not helpful for sellers and why it contributes to the myth.

Before we jump into a discussion of listing agents, we should clear up some confusion about titles. The profession does not really have a title for agents like "listing agent." That is an informal reference to an agent who lists property. But it's also a misnomer, because I don't know of any agent who only lists property and does not also represent buyers. We've all heard of agents advertising as a "Buyer's Agent," but when was the last time you saw an agent advertise as a "Listing Agent"?

We could more accurately refer to a "listing agent" of a particular property. Some agents focus on listings, but they also represent buyers every chance they get. So they act as both listing agents and buyer's agents. Many home sellers think of someone who has a lot of listings as a listing agent. But we will see later that having a lot of listings does not automatically translate to an expertise in marketing and selling properties. For purposes of this discussion, I will still use "listing agent" as many home sellers use the title.

Other agents focus primarily on buyers, and we call them "Buyers' Agents." But this does not mean they don't also list properties from time to time. Anytime an agent represents a buyer while showing homes and drafts an offer on another agent's listing, he is a buyer's agent. There is also a very small segment of the real estate profession who call themselves an "Exclusive Buyer's Agent." They only represent buyers and never list properties.

An agent acts as a Dual Agent when he is the listing agent representing the seller and also represents the buyer on the same property. If a Dual Agent does not reveal any confidential information from one client to the other such that it would compromise one of his clients, then dual agency can work fine if the buyer and seller are both mature and experienced in buying and selling. If they are not, or if one of them is not, one or both of the clients will end up relying on their Dual Agent to come up with the price and terms, who may end up negotiating with himself. That would compromise one or both clients. Honesty and integrity are the keys to a successful dual agency.

The term Realtor® confuses a lot of people. Realtor® is a registered trademark of the National Association of Realtors (NAR), and only dues paying members of NAR can use the title Realtor®. Not all real estate agents are Realtors®. The title is always capitalized.[1]

In Washington State the title for agents recently was changed by law from "agents" to "brokers," so now every agent is a broker. I will use agent and broker interchangeably in this book, because many still think in terms of agents, and in many other states the word "agent" is still used. The change in the law has created some confusion, because for decades "broker" has always referred to the broker in charge at a brokerage or the Designated Broker. Now all agents are brokers. There is another name, the Designated Agent of each office, who is the one broker responsible to the department of licensing for the entire office. And another title you'll see on business cards is Managing Broker. Any broker can call themselves a managing broker, so that title doesn't mean much anymore since they don't have to actually manage anything except themselves.[2]

The Misconception

Now let's get back to the misconception that many home sellers have, that they should list their home with a listing agent, i.e. someone who has a lot of listings. Why would they think that?

The reason most home sellers think they should list with a listing agent is because they are thinking logically that a listing agent has the best marketing system and is advertising to qualified buyers and is the most qualified person to sell their property. There is a general assumption on the part of home sellers that this person can do more for them than anyone else.

Is that true?

Listings, Listings, Listings

Let me lay the foundation that will demonstrate why this is a myth. When I started in real estate in the mid-1970s the real estate gurus were preaching that the name of the game was listings, listings, and listings. One Denver broker who taught at my first continuing education seminar in Fairbanks, Alaska, told us, "I get paid even when I'm on vacation, because I have listings that other agents are selling. Once you have a lot of listings, you make money even if you don't sell anything yourself. That's where the money is folks. Listings, listings, and listings."

After three decades in the business, I can tell you the real estate industry still supports the idea that the name of the game is listings, listings, and listings. <u>Note that the emphasis is not on marketing those listings. The focus is on getting the listings</u>. In other words, the focus is on helping the agent make money, not on marketing and selling your home to the most qualified buyers.[3]

Many top producers are top producers because they simply list a lot of properties. In 90% to 95% of the time listings are sold by other agents, not the listing agent. When a listing agent sells his own listing as a dual agent, he gets to double dip and make twice the commission. So it's a gold mine for him either way. You can see why getting listings is the name of the game for many agents.

When an agent focuses on getting a lot of listings, he is not necessarily focusing on each client's best interests. He is focusing on his business model, which is to list a lot of properties, and as a result to make money even when he fails to sell his own listings himself. So long as an agent has lots of listings, there will be other agents who sell enough of that agent's listings so that he will still make a lot of money.

In other words, an agent can fail to sell your home, but if another agent sells it, your listing agent will still count it as a success. And at his future listing presentations he will tell prospective clients that he sold your home. The truth is, he did not sell your home. He listed it. Another agent sold it.[4]

Office Conversations Among Agents

I think it is important to address what agents say among themselves on this subject. Imagine you are sitting in a real estate brokerage in Anyplace, U.S.A., and you read my statement above that a listing agent who has a listing sold by another agent did not sell that property: he listed it, and the buyer's agent sold it. What would other agents say about that? Here are the kinds of comments you might hear from other agents.

"Of course I sold that listing. It was my listing, and I put it in the MLS, and if another agent sells it while representing the buyer, it still counts as my sale."

"We get to count all sales, whether we are on one end or both ends. Nothing wrong with that."

"It doesn't matter whether I represented the seller or the buyer. If it closes, I made the sale."

These are the kinds of comments you might hear. Most agents see absolutely nothing wrong with claiming they sold a property even if it was another buyer's agent who actually sold it.

They are defining a sale the way they want to, but it is not accurate from a contract law perspective or by the meaning of the words in plain English. The contracts specifically distinguish a listing agent from a selling agent. So does plain English. The MLS does, too.

The truth is that they listed it and another agent sold it. Isn't that really the precise truth? If that isn't the truth, then you will have two agents both claiming they sold a property every time a property closes once.

In other words, agents would be claiming twice as many homes sold as actually sold. And they do that. But the truth is on every sale one agent listed it, and one agent sold it. Or an agent acted as a dual agent and both listed and sold it. But in the latter case, he doesn't get to claim he sold two houses when he only sold one as a dual agent.

Some agents may get confused at this point, because they know that in the MLS if they act as a dual agent, they get credit for both sides. But in the MLS each side represents one-half of a transaction, where one half is the listing side and one half is the selling side. Getting credit for both sides as a dual agent in the MLS for statistical purposes does not also mean they can claim to sell two houses when they only sold one.

I have written elsewhere that a listing agent deserves credit if he marketed a property well, but the credit for actually selling it to a buyer goes to the agent who represented the buyer. If a listing agent deserves credit, he deserves credit for listing it and marketing it well (if he did), but not for selling it. Even the MLS makes a distinction between a listing agent and a selling agent when a property is marked sold.

The Hardest Job is Not Listing

If a listing agent just lists a property and all he does is throw it in the MLS for other agents to sell, then any agent can do that. **Listing is not the hard part—selling is.**

This doesn't mean that doing a good job as a listing agent is easy. It's not when that agent is doing their job marketing that listing. But just throwing a listing in the MLS is easy, especially if the photos are lousy.

Let's see if this triggers an "aha" moment for you. Who impresses you more—the agent that lists a lot of homes and puts them in the MLS for other agents to sell, or the agents who actually sell those homes?

Statistics and the Art of Manipulation

Don't forget to differentiate the statistics an agent gives you. When an agent says he sold X number of homes, you must take that number and subtract all the homes he listed but were sold by other agents. Remember, nearly all agents count their own sold listings as their own sales even if another agent actually sold them. This is commonly accepted practice in the real estate industry.

Be careful, because if you don't know what you're looking at or how to interpret the stats an agent shows you, you can jump to the wrong conclusions. An agent could show you a page of stats from the MLS that shows he is near the top or number X among agents, but is he showing you the number of listings he had that were sold by other agents and by him? Or is he showing you the number of homes he personally sold? Can you see his average selling price? What about his sales volume?

The MLS will pull stats up in a variety of ways, depending on the parameters that were typed in, but be careful because if you don't know how to read the stats, you might believe something that is not precisely true, even if it is generally accepted practice.

For the real estate agent who lives and breathes integrity, success in sales is a byproduct of outstanding performance and loyalty to clients. For agents who focus on numbers and money only, their entire approach uses clients as a means to make money. Everything is different about these two approaches, but they both look very similar in a listing presentation. Ultimately, if you hire the wrong agent you are responsible for the results. If you hire the right agent, you are also responsible for the results.

There Are Great Listing Agents

The truth is the agents who list properties and who make every diligent effort to do their very best in all areas for their clients' sake do not have time to list a gazillion properties. I have many colleagues who are great listing agents, and they are a pleasure to work with.

But there isn't enough time in the week to handle a huge number of listings and have enough time to do what the listing clients expect and **assume** their agents will do.

I just had a conversation with a gentleman who has been very successful. He has bought and sold many houses. He told me what his biggest frustration was with his last listing agent. His complaint is the number one complaint nationwide. What do you think it is?

He said his agent was a nice person, but all she did was list his house and put it in the MLS. According to him, that was it. She didn't communicate with him much either. On top of that she never showed his house, which was her own listing. Other agents were the ones showing it, and he always had to call her to find out what's going on. The significance of this common complaint is greater than meets the eye at first glance.[5]

Apart from proving that some agents do not communicate well with their clients, it makes the bigger point I'm trying to make in this chapter. Notice that the listing agent doesn't show the house. Why? Because she lists, lists, and lists, but she has no marketing system reaching out to qualified buyers.

If she did, she would be showing the house a lot. She listed with the expectation that some agent, any agent, would sell her listing and she doesn't have to do anything, other than put it in the MLS. She doesn't even have time for staying in touch with her own listing client. But when another agent sells it, she will claim she sold it in all her future listing presentations. Does anyone else have a problem with that?

Hundreds of Listings

There are agents who claim to handle hundreds of listings, and I'll share with you exactly how they do that shortly. I think you'll be surprised when I tell you how they do it. Hint: They are not the supermen (or superwomen) they want you to think they are.

For some listing agents, numbers is the name of the game—lots of listings and lots of signs. They will list anything. Why? Because they get to put up a lot of signs, and signs advertise them, and that is free advertising. The more home sellers see a name, the more they **assume** that agent is more capable of selling their property than other agents.

Of course, if a listing agent also has a fantastic marketing system and the knowledge, competence, professionalism, and honesty and integrity you would hope and expect them to have, then listing with him would be good.

Here's a rhetorical question for you. Do you know what a great real estate marketing system looks like today?[6] Would you recognize one if you saw it? If you cannot answer with a strong yes, how will you differentiate listing agents? How will you distinguish hype from reality?

The Revelation

I got a call from a retired couple who wanted to meet with me in their gorgeous home. They had listed their home for a year with another agent. It had not sold, and they shared that there was very little activity, that they did not hear much from their agent, and they didn't get satisfactory answers from their listing agent about what to do next to market their home or how to do it. They came to the conclusion that simply putting it in the MLS was not enough.

I met with them, and they asked me how I do what I do. They found me on the Internet and realized I had the largest Internet presence of any agent they could find on the Olympic Peninsula. After 40 minutes of explaining to them how I sell so many homes and how I connect with so many qualified buyers, the husband had an epiphany and turned to his wife:

> *Honey I know what we've been doing wrong. We were looking for a listing agent when we should have been looking for a buyer's agent like Chuck who actually connects with so many qualified buyers.*[7]

It was a marvelous moment, a moment of truth and revelation. This gentleman had articulated something I knew but had never expressed so clearly.

A home seller today wants an agent who is connecting with qualified buyers and selling a lot of homes himself. The revelation was that traditional listing agents are not necessarily that kind of agent today, if they ever were. This client came to the realization that the ideal listing agent today is most likely a great selling agent who also knows how to list and market.

The more you think about it, the more sense it makes. Why list with someone who just lists properties? Why not list with someone who sells a lot of properties by directly connecting with buyers? That would be like getting both a listing agent and a buyer's agent who finds all the buyers in one package. My argument to home sellers is that I do all the effective things traditional listing agents do (without wasting time and money on what does not work), plus I do a whole lot more marketing to qualified buyers.

Eureka! This is like discovering a hidden secret that few home sellers ever discover. It took me many years to come to this realization myself, but then all of this has been part of the evolutionary changes taking place over many years in the industry. Changes in technology, the Internet, and consumers' changing preferences and habits have made huge leaps, but many of these leaps have not been recognizable at the time. It's only later as we look back that we can see clearly what has happened.

These folks listed their gorgeous home with me, and guess what? Another agent representing the buyer sold it. Hallelujah! Notice I didn't exaggerate and say, "I listed it, and I sold it." I told the truth and said I listed it and another agent sold it. But there is more to the story.

This success was not the result of simply listing

a property and throwing it in the MLS and doing nothing. These buyers specifically revealed that they bought it after viewing the extensive video and photos I took and published all over the Internet, and the articles and sales descriptions (and below the hood all the search engine optimization).

In other words, while another agent represented the buyer in this transaction, the buyer found the home and was persuaded to buy it because of my marketing material and the system I had in place on the Internet that this buyer found by specifically searching for her dream home. The buyer did not find this home because their buyer's agent had a big marketing system.

By the way, the video was not a virtual tour consisting of duplicates of the photos in the MLS. It was real video with my sellers in the video talking about the features of their gorgeous home. Their listing was published in two MLS systems[8], syndicated to hundreds of sites, written about on a powerful and highly ranked real estate blog, and photos, videos, and other resources for buyers were created and broadcast to qualified buyers around the United States.

Multiple websites and blogs and mobile search tools and information were created specifically for qualified buyers. Special SEO (search engine optimization) was used for the specific features of this home so buyers who searched for this exact kind of home would find it. So connecting with this qualified buyer was part of my job as a listing agent, and I did exactly that. There was no luck involved. If anyone was lucky, it was the agent who the buyer called up and asked to write the offer.

Now if I talk about listing that home, I do not ever lead anyone to believe that I also sold it as a buyer's agent. I participated in marketing it so it would get sold, but a buyer's agent sold it. I did my job listing and marketing, but I don't have to exaggerate, and I don't have to try to get home sellers to believe something that is only half true so they will list their homes with me.

This is why I say the traditional dividing line between listing agents and buyers' agents is no longer a valid separation when it comes to choosing and hiring an agent to list and sell your home. Today the most effective listing agent may actually be what some call a buyer's agent, but only because that agent sells so many homes directly to buyers through his own powerful marketing system. That's exactly what you want in a listing agent.

Listing and Selling - Different Skill Sets

Here's an interesting thought for you. I believe the traditional listing agent and the traditional selling agent have different skill sets. Listing agents of the past have not had the marketing and sales skills of selling agents. And selling agents (or buyer's agents) have not had the same requisite skills required to get a lot of listings on a consistent basis.

This theory explains a lot about why traditional listing agents don't do much marketing to qualified buyers. To get a lot of listings, an agent typically does a lot of cold calling, mailings, and hustles people to get their listings. The cold calling involves calling expired listings, withdrawn listings, and may also include calling widows or widowers whose spouses passed away in previous months. There are dozens of techniques to find out who to call. But cold calling requires a certain kind of person or personality.

Selling agents (buyer's agents) are not normally the kind of people who make cold calls. In fact, most of them hate cold calling, so they won't do it. Cold calling, along with some of the other aggressive techniques, are really required if an agent is going to get a lot of listings.

Listing agents who are focused on listings, listings, and more listings, do not really want to build an extensive marketing system to buyers. They do mass mailings, cold calls, and other paid advertising and lead generation, but they don't typically want to spend the time and effort to learn to write extensively, to build Internet marketing sites, and to do extra photos and videos to promote a community.

But a selling agent (buyer's agent) is all about marketing to buyers. He is the kind of personality that thinks night and day about how to connect with the highest qualified buyers. This kind of person also spends a lot of time creating systems behind the scenes to develop relationships with qualified buyers. He also pursues knowledge on marketing and everything related to negotiating and working hard for buyers.

If you think about it, the traditional listing agent and the traditional selling agent (buyer's agent) have completely different skill sets. No wonder so many listing agents focus on listings, listings, and more listings without building a powerful and effective marketing system to connect with highly qualified buyers. And no wonder some listing agents concentrate on building massive systems that focus totally on more and more listings.[9]

The Superman Complex

I promised earlier to tell you how some agents list so many homes and claim credit for all those listings and sales. First, let's all acknowledge it is not humanely possible for one agent to list and effectively manage and market hundreds of homes. Could they do it with assistants and other agents? Yes, if they had a lot of other agents and/or assistants.

More than likely they could do it with a team of people, and that's exactly what they do. They typically put together a team of agents, and put everything under the one agent's name or in the name of the team (which is often the one agent's name). This is exactly how one agent claimed he sold 500 homes in a year, and another agent claimed 1,000.

Many agents around the country are making outrageous sales claims. People who do not know that these agents actually have dozens or even hundreds of agents working under them putting everything in their name or in the name of their teams, assume that these agents are super agents. Solely based on those grossly exaggerated claims, good people list their homes with these super agents assuming these agents have some secret no other agents have. Alas, too many home sellers have not done their homework before hiring an agent. There are no super agents—only guys who look like Clark Kent.

The idea of a "team" in real estate brokerage started as a good idea a couple of decades ago with a husband and wife working together as an effective team, or several friends working together to help each other cover all the bases. It was an excellent way to bring various skills together and combine everyone's calendar to properly manage listings and sell properties. The team concept was a way to work with more clients without losing the importance of keeping the client and the client's best interests at the center of everything.

Unfortunately, there are too many in the real estate business who will abuse good ideas, and the concept of the "team" is one of those. The agents who brag that they sold hundreds of homes have fallen into the trap of grossly exaggerating to make money.

They can argue that such exaggeration is not a violation of the Code of Ethics, but when you hear an agent state, "I sold 500 homes," and when he keeps using the personal pronoun, "I," without even a hint that dozens of agents and assistants work under him, would anyone argue that this is anything other than intentional misrepresentation? Legally and ethically in a courtroom it may not be, but to the average person, is there any doubt the agent intends to convey the impression that he personally sold all those homes by himself? He wants people to think he is Superman.[10]

If an agent came to your house to do his best listing presentation wearing a Superman costume, would you think he is trying to give you the impression he is Superman? Of course, but I doubt you would be fooled.

Do you think that maybe the best listing agent for your home could be a good selling agent? Maybe instead of looking for a traditional listing agent, you should be looking for a buyer's agent (who is a listing agent also), one who sells a lot of homes to qualified buyers. What a novel concept!

I included my ***26 Point Checklist for Interviewing Agents*** as a Bonus Chapter. This checklist is intended as a guide to help you think through the issues that are important to you as you consider hiring and interviewing agents.

---

[1] The term REALTOR® is a registered collective membership mark that identifies a real estate professional who is a member of the National Association of REALTORS® and subscribes to its strict Code of Ethics.

[2] The definitions and responsibilities of brokers in Washington are found in RCW 18.85.011.

[3] Secret No. 2. Listing and marketing homes are not the same thing and rarely performed well by the same agent.

[4] Secret No. 3. This secret can revolutionize your thinking about listing. Almost all agents take credit for sales they did not personally make when another agent sells one of their listings.

[5] Secret No. 4. Most listing agents don't do much beyond listing a property and throwing it in an MLS, and this is after a beautiful listing presentation with a three-ring binder and color glossies.

[6] A powerful marketing system for real estate is incredible when you get to see the big picture and all the pieces working smoothly together to produce consistent results. It is beyond the scope of this book to lay out the precise

business model and full marketing plan of my own brokerage, iRealty Virtual Brokers. That would require a large book of its own. Of course, I won't be giving all my "patented" technologies, strategies, and methods away to other agents free anytime soon. This book shares what is essentially the tip of the iceberg of a massive marketing system.

[7] Secret No. 5. Look for a great agent who is connecting with buyers when you list your home, not a listing agent who just lists property for other agents to sell.

[8] The Olympic Listing Service (OLS) is the MLS used in Clallam County, Washington, and is a service called Paragon, owned by a large financial services company, Black Knight Financial Services, based in Jacksonville, Florida. The Northwest MLS service is the second MLS available in the Sequim and Port Angeles area, and is the largest MLS in the State of Washington used by all the agents in the Seattle and Tacoma metropolitan area as well as most of the counties in the state. The NWMLS is owned by its member agents and is based in Kirkland, Washington.

[9] This theory that listing agents and selling agents have different skill sets was a brilliant revelation, and I cannot take the credit. One of my clients shared this idea with me, and as soon as he did, I knew it hit the nail right on the head. Thank you Phil.

[10] Secret No. 6. Take a page from a lesson you've learned in your own life, namely, if it seems too good to be true, it probably is. Be cautious of agents who claim to be number one, or who claim to sell dozens of homes or even hundreds of homes per year. Remember, there are no Supermen or Super-women. Some have learned to game the system to look better than they really are.

Myth 3
List With the Highest Bidder

There is one trap that catches far too many home sellers, and too many pay a hefty price in lost market time and smaller net proceeds at closing. And it's all so unnecessary. Here's how it happens.

A homeowner met with three real estate agents from different offices to find out what their home was worth, and to interview the agents to decide which one would be their listing agent. All three agents were nice and had good presentations.

One had a very impressive three ring binder with gorgeous color glossies and a pitch that emphasized the size of the brokerage. The goal of the presentation was to dazzle the home seller with the success of the brokerage on a national level, and to use the power of proven visual aides. The presentation was a template that the franchise encouraged all their agents to use. It was good, but the home seller was left with an undefined feeling that something was missing.

It may have been that the agent was selling the national brokerage and neglected to bring personal experience and credibility to the table.

The next agent had a nice presentation with color slides, charts, and data on a laptop (or iPad). This presentation was largely data driven with the goal of "proving" to the home seller that she should list with this agent. While the charts and graphs were well done, it was probably too much detailed information, and the home seller felt the agent seemed a little cold or mechanical during the presentation. Again the home seller just didn't get that "aha" moment in which she was convinced this person should be her listing agent.

The last agent had no three ring binder and no fancy slide show on a laptop, but seemed to be the most knowledgeable and was very friendly. The presentation almost seemed too simple without all the fancy charts and slides, although there was plenty of solid content and examples. It was more personal and gave the home seller deeper insight into the agent himself. But for the home seller, there didn't seem to be any big persuasive closing point.

Which of these three agents should win the listing?

We cannot decide based on that meager information. The best listing agent might be the one with-out any presentation material, or one of the others. One has to look beyond the presentation to the sub-stance. There is much more to consider, but do you know what single factor seems to consistently sway the majority of home sellers, and what determines which agent they will hire?

The Biggest Winner of Listings

Which agent gets the listing almost every time? The answer, as simple as it sounds, is the highest bid-der. I know what you're thinking. You're thinking that's just plain silly. Home sellers are smart, discerning, and they know how to hire an agent. You would be right if you said home sellers are smart, but not all home sellers know how to discern the difference between agents.

Here's the scenario. The three agents all did their presentations, and each gave the home seller a number, which represented the theoretical listing price. One agent quoted a price of $299,900, another quoted a price of $325,000, but the third agent took a different approach. He said with total confidence, "No doubt about it, I can sell your home for $385,000. I have buyers now on a waiting list. Yep. I just sold a home very similar to yours down the street for $392,500, and it didn't have the nice deck yours has. Just yesterday I had one of my buyers describe the home they were looking for, and they described your home. Yep. I think we can get $385,000, maybe a little less in the negotiations, but that's where we should start."

The vast majority of home sellers will go with the highest bidder at $385,000. Who wouldn't want more money? But the property sits in the MLS for three months without much, if any, action, at which time the listing agent recommends reducing the price to $369,000. Another three months goes by, and the listing agent recommends another price reduction to $349,000. Now six months have passed.

The home seller is wanting to move on and be done with waiting and waiting for a buyer and constantly having to have their home ready for viewing on short notice, so they call their listing agent and asked what can be done. Their listing agent recommends another price reduction, this time to $329,000.

At this point this home has been on the market for almost a year. It started at $385,000, and now it is listed at $329,000. A lot of market time has been lost, and during the recession, prices often continued to go down. So this strategy cost a lot of home sellers tens of thousands of dollars during the recession.

When an offer does finally come in, it is for $295,000. The home seller is not happy. That's a long way from $385,000. They will take a loss at $295,000, and that won't leave nearly as much as they need to buy their next home. Their listing agent recommends a counteroffer to meet the buyer halfway, which is about $315,000. The buyer counters again halfway at $307,500. The sellers grapple with this price, and they grind their teeth all night long. The next day, their listing agent tells them if they don't accept this offer, their house could be on the market for another year. They accept $307,500.

So guess who had the most honest listing presentation? The agent who proposed $325,000. And there is a very good probability that had it been listed at $325,000 in the very beginning, it would have sold within several months, and that the selling price would have been higher than $307,500. A home on the market for a long time grows stale. Buyers who saw it walked away because it was initially overpriced. They moved on and bought other homes. That means this home lost potential buyers during the overpriced listing period. In addition, during a recession, prices can drop even further over time. Ultimately, a home will often sell for less than what it could have gotten had it been marketed properly from the beginning at a more realistic listing price.

Do not conclude from this story that the best listing agent is always in the middle. Do not conclude that the best listing agent is the lowest or the highest bidder either. You have to discern more about an agent and his approach to marketing your home.

It's extremely hard to know if you're getting good listing presentations that are all realistic, or whether you are getting two good listing presentations and a third one full of hype. It's very hard to discern the difference. This is why I harp on honesty and professional integrity so much.

The Lowest Bidder

There's a variation of the above scenario, and it involves the lowest bidder. Every once in a while, a listing agent will low ball a home seller on the listing price. It's the kind of price that sells the house in the first few days or weeks. I just met with a California client who told me he bought his last home in California for $50,000 less than he would have paid had it been priced competitively. He walked into a house that was just listed, and he offered full listing price on the first day. He told me the listing agent did a disservice to his own client, because the house was easily worth $50,000 more than the listing price, and he would have paid that. That was almost 10% of its value.

Traps for The Unwary

There is another trap, but this is one that some

home sellers create for themselves and their agents. This may or may not surprise you.

Some home sellers are very strong personalities, and while that is perfectly fine, some of these personalities will tell, not ask, a professional and competent and honest agent what the listing price will be. Every agent has had clients like this. They are good people, honest, hard working, successful, and wonderful in a hundred ways. But they don't have the experience of a full time agent who has been in the business for decades, and they don't look at hundreds of homes, and they aren't selling homes every month and working with buyers every week.

There clearly is such a thing as knowing just enough to be dangerous. The problem for this kind of home seller is that when it comes to selling their home they are dangerous to themselves, and they don't even know it. They "know" what their home is worth and what a buyer should pay. And it's not really open for discussion.

In some cases it's not that a home seller knows what their home is worth, it's that they know what they "must net." I've had clients tell me what they needed to net, as if that had anything to do with fair market value or what buyers will pay. The way they told me left absolutely no room for discussion on what

I felt it should be listed for.

Imagine a seller saying with a strong raised voice, "I won't sell it for less than X. No by God, I'm not going there. I'll keep the damn house before I give it away." What's an agent to say? When a client talks like that and their face is red or they've raised their voice while pressing the point and letting the agent know how strongly they feel about their bottom line, they are not asking or encouraging any response at all from the agent. They are telling the agent.

In a small market where you don't have mathematical proof a home should be listed for less, it's a lost cause to get into an argument with an adamant seller. So a good listing agent can find himself in a bad situation, because a home seller absolutely insists that the home be listed higher than the agent's gut feeling says it should be.

Later this can backfire on the cooperative listing agent, because when the listing expires and the home hasn't sold, the home seller wants to list with a new agent who always wants to reduce the price. And then later the home sells at a lower price. The home seller thinks the original listing agent was no good. Every agent experiences this kind of scenario, and it is frustrating.

This is very hard for an agent, even the best of

agents. Assume the true fair market value of a home is $350,000. And let's say a prospective agent suggests $359,000 after studying the comps and a host of data. If the seller adamantly says it should be listed at $450,000, what is the agent to do? He cannot prove mathematically that it is only worth $359,000, or any other number. No matter how many comps he might show the seller, the seller may come back firm at $450,000. The seller could be right, or he might be way off. A CMA (comparative market analysis) or even a formal appraisal is still nothing but an educated guess about what a buyer will pay.

An agent often feels like he is smashing his head against a concrete wall when he deals with a strong personality who insists on an excessively high listing price. Ultimately, the agent will often be forced to list it too high, or to simply walk away. The problem with walking away is that some other agent will list it at $450,000. Then the price gets reduced multiple times as the home seller realizes it must be over time, and ultimately the home sells a year later for $339,000. Guess who earns the commission? The later agent, not the first agent who knew what he was talking about and walked rather than list too high. So sometimes even good agents accept an overpriced listing, because they know how that can play out.

Myth 4
Every Agent Has the Best System

This chapter was inspired by a woman in her eighties. She had her home listed for sale, and I showed it to one of my buyers. She couldn't leave, so I met her briefly as I showed her lovely home. She was a widow, and the home was just too much for her to maintain. She was proud of her home, and she also told me she liked her listing agent, who told her he was "all over the Internet."

Why did she mention that? Because she said her daughter, who lives in California, told her to make sure she gets a listing agent who has a good Internet marketing system. I presume she asked her agent at the listing presentation if he was on the Internet, and he must have given her the answer she obviously wanted, "I'm all over the Internet. Oh yea. All over the Internet."

Of course, she didn't check to see if he was all over the Internet. I'm sure she did not know how to check these things. I've interviewed a lot of homeowners over the years, and I can tell you that home sellers rarely, if ever, actually check what listing agents tell them.

I didn't say much, except to be polite. I remember thinking at the time, if her listing agent is all over the Internet, I'm Dick Tracy. I don't care what other agents do or don't do. I'm busy enough babysitting myself without trying to babysit anyone else. But I do care about widows and widowers and the elderly, and I care about whether they are treated honestly and fairly.

All of this is important, because as the title of this chapter suggests, *"Every Agent Has The Best System."* I cannot tell you how many sellers have told me that more than one agent they interviewed said they have the best marketing system. Can you imagine being a seller who interviews three agents, and all three look you right in the eyes and say, "I have the largest marketing system of any agent in the area." This kind of exaggeration is getting out of control. No wonder home sellers are skeptical.[1]

Here's a true story. I listed a home that had been listed with another agent for almost a year, and the home sellers were not very pleased with their agent. Okay, I get that. That can happen even when an agent does a good job, right? Sometimes personalities don't click, and sometimes no matter how much an agent does right, they never get along well with their client during the term of the listing. The sellers told me their story, even though I did not ask. I could tell it was therapeutic for them to be able to share their story. So without interrupting, I patiently listened.

Their listing agent had used several outdated marketing strategies during the term of the listing, and their agent did not have any significant Internet marketing system that reached out directly to qualified buyers. The relationship had not gone smoothly. It's good to under promise and over deliver, but it can be devastating to over promise and under deliver. They told me that their listing agent had made promises she could not or did not keep. While she may not have claimed she had the best marketing system, they listed with her because they thought she and her brokerage had one of the best, if not the best marketing system.

There is another mistake that I think many agents make, and this is a personal opinion with plenty of room for differences of opinion. When home sellers are unhappy, frustrated, or even angry with their listing agents, they will often ask to be released from their listing contract so they can list with another agent, or sell their home as a FSBO. The tragic mistake so many agents make is telling their clients that they cannot get out of their contract until the expiration date. Big mistake in my humble opinion.

I know, having been a real estate lawyer, that a contract is a contract, and an agent can tell a seller they are stuck with them until the contract expires (with an exception I will discuss later), but it is not a wise approach, certainly not one that Dale Carnegie would have endorsed after writing his book *How to Win Friends and Influence People*.

Even if an agent did a truly outstanding job during the listing, and his clients don't understand that, and they want to be released from their contract, how much sense does it make to force a client to stick it out for the remainder of the contract?

If a client is unhappy for any reason or no reason at all, why not just say, "I understand. I have enjoyed working with you, but I also want you to be able to do what you feel is best for you, so how soon would you like me to terminate the listing and take it out of the MLS? I could do it today or anytime you prefer."

Taking it out of the MLS is easy. It doesn't take days or weeks. It only takes about 30 seconds to remove it from the MLS as an active listing. If the agent wants a termination agreement in writing and signed, he can do that in the days following.

What compounds the offense to sellers is that

their request to have the contract terminated may be morally and legally justified. What an offense it is to the seller when they believe they are legally justified in terminating the listing agreement and their agent is demanding that they sign another contract to terminate, a contract in which the agent takes no responsibility for breaching the contract and in which the client seems to be the one blamed. What do I mean by the agent breaching the contract?

There is a scenario in which a home seller is legally entitled to termination of a listing contract prior to the expiration date. In Washington State there have been many cases addressing this issue, and judges have repeatedly ruled that a home seller is entitled to termination of the contract when an agent has not performed under the contract. In other words, when an agent has not done all they promised and contracted to do, the agent has breached the listing contract, and the home seller is entitled to terminate the contact.

How could a listing agent breach his legal duties? It happens when an agent does not market a property to buyers, when he doesn't present offers in a timely manner, when he reveals confidential information, and when he breaches any of the duties under state law. In Washington those duties are spelled out in the Revised Code of Washington and interpreted by

State courts. [See a partial list at the end of this chapter.][2]

I think that the majority of agents do not understand that they can breach the listing agreement. Too many listing agents get a seller to sign a listing, and the agent puts it in the MLS, but if that's all they do, they could be in substantial breach of their duties and obligations under the terms of the listing agreement and state law.

Mistreating a client when the agent may be the one in breach of the listing contract is just daring the client to sue the agent and the agent's brokerage, and the agent's errors and omission insurance company, for breach of contract and violations of the consumer protection act, and to file a written complaint with the Department of Licensing, the local real estate association, the state association, and the national association, and to file a complaint with the attorney general's office, with the Better Business Bureau, and to start a negative Internet campaign.

Clearly, it is not worth going down that path. I seriously don't think agents are thinking this through when they tell their clients, "No, you have no right to terminate the contract until it expires, and you will work with me no matter what until then." Not a good idea. I'm just saying.

Perhaps agents get greedy, or perhaps they just don't understand how to build and maintain positive relationships with clients, but many certainly do not know how to diplomatically end a relationship without making it much worse. Some agents don't just burn bridges behind them, they blow them up.

Open House Disaster

I was surprised to hear of a listing agent who held multiple open houses in a community where the buyers are retirees from other states. What are the chances that one of those buyers would be in town on the exact day of the open house? What are the odds that buyers would even know about the open house if they were here? What are the odds it would be the house that buyers from out of town wanted?

In a healthy real estate market the NAR (National Association of Realtors®) reported that less than 2% of homes sell at open houses. Turn that around, and here's what that means. At least 98% of open houses do not sell because of the open house. I don't know about you, but I have never operated my business or my life based on a 98% failure rate.

The good folks listed with this agent because they thought she had the best marketing system. She not only did not have the best, she was operating out of a 20 year old marketing plan that was broken.

You Hire One Agent, Not a Building

Let me share a little secret full of common sense. When you hire a listing agent, you hire one individual, not a team, not the senior company executives, not the entire building of agents, and not the bricks-and-mortar itself. You hire one individual named in your listing contract. That's it. This is especially true of franchises. A local franchise office is run by locals, and **listing your property always boils down to one person working for you.**[3]

In fact, the bureaucracy and dated systems of a franchise or a large bricks-and-mortar brokerage can actually get in the way of effective marketing. I have worked for some big brokerages in my career, and I have first hand experience with this. I've written a book, *The New World of Marketing For Real Estate Agents*, that explains this in detail and why consumers are no longer being served by the big corporations in the sky.

The best agents in the country are just as likely to work for themselves or a small boutique brokerage as they are for the largest brokerage. Why? Because knowledge, experience, competence, professionalism, hard work, honesty, and integrity are personal characteristics, not corporate. Only individuals can possess these values.

For individual agents at the large franchises,

they cannot do just anything they want. They are stuck with volumes of three-ring binders full of rules and regulations telling agents what they can and cannot do. Many agents discover they cannot just go out and start doing their own powerful Internet marketing to advertise their listings and connect with the most qualified buyers using the latest SEO (search engine optimization), videos, articles, and social media. They have to get permission, and sometimes permission will be denied. These companies cannot have agents all doing their own thing when the corporation is trying to strictly control the brand.

The truth is, the corporation is trying to control something else, too. The corporation's business model demands that they control all the agents' marketing systems and all the leads, and ownership of all the listings belongs to the corporations too. For many agents, this is like wearing a straight jacket when it comes to building their business and doing what they know is most effective for their clients.

Many agents have been leaving the franchises. They are tired of being in a monstrous bureaucracy, and they are tired of being told they cannot do this or that. But they are also tired of giving away so much of their commissions and getting nickel and dimed on other small costs. As a result, the culture of the large brokerages is too often one that demands that agents continue with old traditional approaches and worn out marketing techniques.

How Much Do Agents Spend on Advertising?

I am going to speculate that the average listing agent spends an average of $200 per listing on advertising during the entire term of a listing. This number comes from a lifetime in the business talking to hundreds of agents over the years. Obviously, some agents will spend more on some "special" listings, and less on others, and some agents spend more per listing than other agents. Seattle luxury home brokers clearly will spend a lot more. One ad in a nationwide luxury real estate magazine can cost several thousand dollars alone.

How much should an agent spend? There is no formula, and the best agents have budgets that vary substantially on how much they spend per listing. There are many factors, such as the length of the listing, the type of property, the price range, the prospective buyers, the location of the property and the location of the most qualified buyers, the state of the real estate market, the client's motivation, and so on.

Ultimate Responsibility

The last lesson in this story is that every home seller bears ultimate responsibility for who they hire to be their listing agent. You and you alone hire your listing agent. You are the principal, and the agent is your agent. Agency law is clear on the responsibilities. You are the boss, and your agent acts only with your authority, and everything your agent does is attributed to you. In other words, you own the success or failure of your listing agent.

If your listing agent does an incredible job marketing your property, and his system and his efforts generate a number of showings, and if he sells your home as a dual agent to a highly qualified buyer, then you can claim credit. If his excellent marketing connects with a buyer who hires their own buyer's agent, and you sell your home, your agent was successful. Your agent is acting on your behalf. His success is your success. You can take credit.

If your listing agent fails to sell your home, if your listing agent does a lousy job marketing your property, if your listing agent is unprofessional or incompetent, you own it all. You and you alone bear the responsibility of doing your due diligence and finding out who the best listing agent is for you. You can blame your listing agent all you want, but I will still ask you, "Didn't you do your own research and interview and hire that agent?"

Here's where most home sellers will say, "Right, I get that, but I don't know how to discern who is knowledgeable, competent, professional, and honest, and how can I know who knows how to market to qualified buyers? Agents all talk alike, so how am I supposed to know who to hire?"

I have the answer, but before I share it, we need to mention a very important way that agents market themselves to people, and many consumers hire their agents this way. You will recognize the names Zillow, Trulia, Realtor.com, Angie's List, Yelp, and other similar services. Real estate agents pay a fortune to advertise on some of these sites, particularly on Zillow and Trulia.

That's all fine and dandy, but do you think for a minute that an agent who pays a lot of money to advertise and show up all over Zillow or Trulia is automatically qualified? Of course not. All it takes is money to advertise on Zillow or Trulia. So here's the rhetorical question, "Why would people simply hire an agent without any serious due diligence just because they show up on those sites?" A lot of money is at stake--your money. Would you trust someone with a few hundred thousand of your hard earned dollars without screening them?

The agent·who gets a lot of leads from Zillow or Trulia would argue that he has a lot of testimonials, and that's proof he is good. It's proof of something, but it's not proof that agent is knowledgeable, competent, professional, honest, and practices with integrity 24/7. He may be, but showing up on those sites proves nothing except that he spent money, and maybe he spent time inputting his profile and information and testimonials.

I like a good testimonial as much as the next guy, and I have many, but even those can be manipulated. I've never manipulated a testimonial, but how hard would it be? On October 6, 2014 Fox News reported that a Craigslist poster was advertising that he would pay $7 to everyone who would post a fake recommendation for a business. No surprise, right?

How to Do Your Own Research

I strongly recommend doing your own first hand research. That means you have to look deeper. You have to know what to look for and where to look. That is why I created a comprehensive due diligence checklist.

Use this checklist, and you won't have to rely on other sources you cannot verify. You won't have to hope someone really does have the largest marketing system. You won't have to hope someone is telling you the exact truth without exaggeration or gaming statistics. You won't have to guess who to hire. You will know which agents are qualified, and you will hire the one in whom you have the greatest confidence. And then you can let your agent do what he does best without breathing down his neck wondering if he knows what the heck he is doing.

You'll find my 26 Point Interview Checklist in the Bonus Section of this book.

---

[1] Secret No. 8. A great listing agent is one who has a great marketing system to qualified buyers for a home in your price range. Don't be fooled into listing with someone who doesn't.

[2] These are some of the legal duties a listing agent owes his client:

To exercise reasonable skill and care;

To deal honestly and in good faith;

To present all written offers, written notices and other written communications to and from either party in a timely manner, regardless of whether the property is subject to an existing contract for sale or the buyer is already a party to an existing contract to purchase;

To disclose all existing material facts known by the broker and not apparent or readily ascertainable to a party;

To account in a timely manner for all money and property received from or on behalf of either party;

To provide a pamphlet on the law of real estate agency;

To be loyal to the seller by taking no action that is adverse or detrimental to the seller's interest in a transaction;

To timely disclose to the seller any conflicts of interest;

To advise the seller to seek expert advice on matters relating to the transaction that are beyond the agent's expertise;

Not to disclose any confidential information from or about the seller, except under subpoena or court order, even after termination of the agency relationship; and

Unless otherwise agreed to in writing after the seller's agent has complied with RCW 18.86.030(1)(f), to make a good faith and continuous effort to find a buyer for the property; except that a seller's agent is not obligated to seek additional offers to purchase the property while the property is subject to an existing contract for sale.

[3] Secret No. 9. When you hire a listing agent, you hire one person, not a building and not a staff. You only hire one person who is responsible, so choose one agent carefully and forget about buildings and branding.

Myth 5
If It Doesn't Sell,
Try Something Different

What do the vast majority of home sellers say when they are unhappy with their current listing agent, and they have decided to list with another agent (or become a FSBO)? "We want to try something different." I guarantee that's what almost every seller says, because they are trying to be polite and not cast aspersions, and the nice way most people say their agent sucks is, "We want to try something different."

After talking with many unhappy home sellers over three decades, I have learned why they want to list with another agent, and the comments are pretty much the same.

> Our listing agent gave us a great listing presentation and made a lot of promises, and he (or she) had a nice looking marketing plan and the whole brokerage sounded so impressive. But after we listed, nothing much happened. There was an open house for other agents, but those

agents flew through the house like their pants were on fire, and for months nothing happened except a couple of showings. Those showings didn't amount to anything, and one of those buyers didn't even want a home like ours. I don't know why the agent even showed it to them. We saw our home in the MLS, and there was some kind of virtual tour consisting of photographs actually, but other than showing up on Zillow and Trulia, nothing really happened. There were some inaccuracies in the information about our property on some of the sites. We emailed our agent, but she was not very responsive, and we called a few times, but never got satisfactory answers to the questions we had about marketing. We wanted to know what we need to do next in terms of marketing, but she didn't seem to know. Basically all our agent did was put our home in the MLS, and that's pretty much it. Our agent is nice, but we're pretty disappointed. So we've decided we want to do something different.

Who wouldn't empathize with these home sellers? That kind of scenario, which often lasts for a year, is stressful without a happy ending. That kind of experience is better than a poke in the eye with a sharp stick, but not by much.[1]

You know how children will ask a question, and when you answer it, they ask, "Why?" And when you answer that, they ask why again? You've got to love the innocent naïveté of children as well as their curiosity to get to the bottom of everything. Home sellers would do well to pick up that pattern by asking why a home is not getting showings and then to ask why it hasn't gotten offers and then to ask why to every answer, and then to dig deeper still on the marketing, both traditional marketing and Internet marketing. Even then sometimes we ask the wrong questions. ***The answers you get are only as good as the questions you ask***.

What is The Fundamental Problem?

So what is the fundamental problem with this home seller's dilemma? Is the problem their listing agent? Maybe, but let's go deeper. Is it the brokerage? Maybe, but let's go deeper. Is it the advertising in the local paper, or is it the open houses, or is it the whole marketing plan? It could be one of these, or it could be all of them, but answering these questions still does not get to the fundamental problem.

There is no doubt there are great agents out there, and yes there are agents that are not so great. Welcome to planet Earth. So if you hire an agent who is not so great, what is the cause of the problem when your home does not sell?

The fundamental problem is the seller's hiring criteria. Many sellers do not know what to look for in a listing agent, but they get exactly the kind of agent and brokerage they hire, and they get exactly the kind of marketing plan that agent uses with all their clients.

Imagine Boeing needing more design engineers who have a specialty in navigation electronics. Would you expect them to know exactly what they need, and to interview prospective engineers who have a resume and history of success doing exactly what they need? Of course. Boeing human resources would know precisely what experience and credentials they needed, and that is exactly what they would look for in their next employee. They would not hire someone unqualified for the position.

A school district that has an opening for a high school special ed teacher would know precisely what it needed, and the job description would be quite specific. Job applicants would be screened first for the right resume and references and other written support, and then they would be interviewed with one goal in mind —can this individual accomplish the goals we set for this position and for the school district?

The Weakest Link

In over three decades in the real estate business, I have come to the conclusion that the single weakest link for home sellers is their lack of understanding about what credentials they need in a listing agent, and how to find that person. Of course, there are home sellers who know exactly what they are looking for and how to filter agents to find the best one, but those sellers are in the minority. The majority of home sellers know a lot about a lot of things, but hiring a qualified real estate agent is not one of them.

If you don't know exactly what you need in a listing agent, your interviews of several agents will boil down to who tells the best story. Talk about being out at sea without a rudder. How are you supposed to make an intelligent decision if you have no criteria upon which to make the decision?

So let's get back to the home seller who had their home listed for a year, and now they want to try something different, meaning they want to "try a different listing agent." How do you know which agent to try the second time if you didn't know the first time?

And if you don't know what criteria to use to make your decision, how do you know if your first agent should be fired? If your first agent lived up to all the important criteria, and your home didn't sell, then it isn't your agent's fault. If your agent actually has the best marketing system, and if your agent is knowledgeable, professional, competent, and honest, why would you want to "try something different" when that probably means listing with a less experienced, less knowledgeable, and less professional agent with a lesser marketing system?

On the other hand, if your listing agent lacked what you need, then you probably should try something different, if trying something different means hiring the right agent this time.

I've seen home sellers make two big mistakes. The first mistake is to hire the wrong agent to begin with. And that mistake is often compounded by hiring the wrong agent the second time they list. The second mistake is an unnecessary one. If they hired the right agent by luck the first time, they often fire him to try something different. In both cases, they feel like they got bad agents, but the only bad thing was that the home seller did not know precisely what they needed in an agent, and they didn't know how to find that person.

The key to avoiding these nightmare scenarios is to know precisely what criteria you need in a listing agent. Easier said then done, but that's what this book is about, helping you know what to look for and what to avoid.

Try something different if you know what kind of agent you need, but don't try something different if you're still shooting from the hip and just guessing what you need in an agent. Trial and error is not the best approach when it comes to selling your home.

---

[1] Secret No. 10. The vast majority of home sellers do not know how to evaluate or interview a listing agent.

Myth 6
Just Keep Reducing the Price

I'll never forget the first time I heard this crazy scenario. A gentleman I knew called me up to ask me a question. He had his home listed with a hot shot real estate agent, and he told me his agent said he should reduce the price on his home every week until it sells. I didn't think my friend was serious, but he insisted that's what his listing agent told him.

The question for me was, "Is this true? Is it a good idea to reduce my listing price every week until it sells?" My answer came with a question, "Before we talk about price, do you think your home has been marketed to qualified buyers?" His immediate answer was, "No." My response was, "Then why are we talking about reducing the price?"

He had an expensive home, and I was just imagining reducing the price every week until he sold it for $1.00. What an incredibly ridiculous marketing approach. Talk about simplicity without any effective marketing strategy! Let's just put your listing in the MLS and reduce the price every week until it sells! It is one of the most reckless marketing approaches I have ever heard of, and it completely disregards the client's best interests.

Too many listing agents across America have taken the approach that "*listings*" is the name of the game, so they list a lot of homes, throw them in the MLS, and then wait for other agents to sell them. If they get lucky, a buyer will come directly to them and they double their commission. But that would be lucky, because they don't have a substantive marketing system to qualified buyers. But with their approach, they don't need a creative and powerful marketing system. All they need to do is list, list, and list. With enough listings, some are bound to get sold by other agents, and the commissions will come rolling in.

With that kind of simplistic business model, they have to have simplistic answers to maintain their listings, because anything that would take time, money or additional marketing is out of the question. So the easiest answer is "reduce the price."

Reducing the price is the right thing to do if a home is listed above its true fair market value, but just to keep reducing the price until it sells is not a rational marketing approach. Keep reducing the price and eventually everything will sell, but what a poor strategy.[1]

The effectiveness of reducing the price is also dependent on the local real estate market and who the ideal buyer is likely to be. Let me explain.

If you're in a market where 75% of the homes sold are basic 3 bedroom, 2 bath homes for young to middle aged couples, priced from $200,000 to $285,000 in subdivisions with small lots, and one hundred of these homes are selling every month, then reducing the price if a home doesn't sell within a reasonable period of time would make sense. Tacoma would be a good example of this kind of market scenario.

But if you're in a market in a small rural area where there are not very many sales, especially for unique homes, and if your home is in the upper price range of homes selling in your market, then price is one factor in getting it sold.

The first and certainly major factor is connecting with that one unique buyer who wants your home. If your most qualified and best buyer is a retiree from California or Colorado or elsewhere, then connecting with that qualified buyer (since they are few and far between in a very small market) will be largely dependent on when that person is retiring or making their move to your area.

This is a factor over which you have no control. Consider this. If you have a great marketing system, but buyers for your home in your small town are few and far between, then the prospective buyer must retire and be looking for homes like yours in an area like yours before anything can happen. Timing is everything.

For example, if that perfect buyer is living in Santa Barbara, and he is retiring twelve months from now and has a plan to start looking for his home on-line six months from now, you can reduce the price every week between now and then, and it will have no affect at all on him or his timeline, nor will it affect anyone else if no one is looking for a home like yours in your area. Reducing the price without a good marketing system and without taking into consideration when and where buyers are is incredibly immature.

Who pays the price of a bad marketing strategy? You do. The agent suffers no loss at all, and constantly reducing the price increases the chances of him making a commission without any additional effort. But you can lose money if the marketing of your home is not reaching the most qualified buyers in your price range.

A good marketing plan is intelligent. It is based on effective marketing and proven advertising techniques. It focuses on connecting with qualified buyers.

It is strategic and implemented with an understanding of the market and who the buyers are in your market. The greatest marketing plan does not guarantee a sale, but it is one heck of a lot better than shooting from the hip and guessing, and it is better than just reducing the price every week until your home sells.

---

[1] Secret No. 11. Reducing the listing price is a good idea only after you have established after a sufficient period of time that your home has been effectively marketed to qualified buyers. Too many people just keep reducing the price without addressing the marketing issue.

Myth 7
It's Easy to Sell Your Own Home Today

Is it easy to sell your own home today? I think most people would admit that it's not. The next question is more difficult. Can you sell your own home today?

Let's do a reality check up front. About 85% of all FSBOs end up listing with an agent because they fail. Of the remaining 15%, a very small percentage get sold, and the larger remainder is taken off the market because they can't sell their homes. Statistically FSBOs are a disaster, but let's take a closer look at what happens and why.

I met a man the other day who said he sold four homes himself during his lifetime. He is a very capable and smart man, but even he would admit that when he sold those homes over the past four decades, those were different times and different real estate markets in different parts of the country. When the market is super hot, all you have to do is whisper, "home for sale," and it gets sold. But those kinds of markets are very rare.

In a normal market, and certainly in a recession, for those of us who are seasoned real estate professionals, we know that a For-Sale-By-Owner (FSBO) has huge disadvantages for some very important reasons. These are solid reasons, and my experience goes back almost four decades in three different states. You may be tempted to say something like, "He's just saying that[1] because he's a Realtor." I am a Realtor, but that doesn't mean I'm wrong about FSBOs and the challenges they face.

Before we jump into why a FSBO is so hard to sell, let's address the two major reasons home sellers decide to sell their own homes. The first and most common reason is that they have had bad experiences with real estate agents. I get that! We've all heard the stories, and there are plenty of them. I was a real estate attorney for 20 years, and I've heard more stories than I care to recall. The answer to getting burned by a real estate agent is not to become a FSBO.

The second reason many decide to become a FSBO is to save the commission. It just doesn't work out like most think it will for many reasons, and the reasons that[2] follow will demonstrate that. It turns out the commission is the least of a seller's concerns today.

The FSBO Disadvantages for the Seller

The first big challenge for a FSBO is reaching qualified buyers.

Marketing real estate to qualified buyers today is not the same as it was 20 years ago, or even 10 years ago or even 5 years ago. You can't just run an ad in the Sunday issue of your local paper and sell your home. That used to work. Now buyers from out of state rarely read the local newspaper, and even the majority of locals don't read the print newspapers anymore, especially when it comes to real estate. As soon as you buy a newspaper, it's out of date. The Internet and live cable news are responsible for that.

A FSBO will not show up in all the major places buyers search. They won't be in the multiple listing service, which means they won't show up on the hundreds of broker sites showing all the local listings. This also means they won't show up on all the syndicated sites that are fed with the IDX data feeds from the local MLS services. This alone ought to give a FSBO pause, but most FSBO's are not aware of this. Imagine choosing to have your home <u>not</u> show up as a listing in this massive network of MLS sites broadcast all over hundreds of sites and getting exposed to tens of thousands of potential buyers.

There are some MLS sites that allow a FSBO to enter their listing for a fee, but not in Washington State and not in most states. Even in states where MLSs permit FSBO listings for a fee, those kinds of listings get no promotion and real estate agents basically ignore those listings. For all practical purposes FSBOs are invisible to buyers.

There are a small number of brokers around the country who will post a FSBO in their MLS for a flat fee. Those services tend to be virtually invisible to buyers, too. I've talked to many sellers who tried that FSBO approach, and they were extremely unhappy with what they got, or did not get. I'm being polite here, because 100% of the people I talked to were angry, not just unhappy with those services. That approach is almost a guaranteed failure.

No matter where a FSBO tries to advertise, he will not get the effort or exposure of hundreds of local agents who are showing homes every day. No one will be talking about this home, writing about it, sharing photos of the property, nor will agents be wanting to show it, even if the owner has promised a selling commission.

I've talked to many FSBOs over the years who all said they would be willing to pay a 2.5% or even a 3% selling agent's commission. Let me see if I can explain how real estate agents feel about that kind of offer.

Imagine you were going to have a baby, or your wife was going to have a baby. You decide to use a midwife instead of a traditional doctor, and you're going to have the delivery in the quiet comfort of your own home. So you call a doctor who specializes in delivering babies, and you tell him you are having a baby at home with a midwife, and you would be glad to pay for the doctor's prescription for some pain medication if he would write it for you when you need it. How do you think the doctor would feel about that?

He might be polite and tell you to come in for an exam, but he won't write a prescription for a midwife so long as he is not delivering. He makes his living delivering babies, not writing prescriptions for midwives. He would undoubtedly consider the whole exchange a bit offensive.

A full time real estate agent supports his family and feeds his children, keeps a roof over his head, and works very hard to be the experienced professional he is. He takes continuing education classes to learn and to be able to renew his license with the state. He pays for errors and omissions insurance, and state fees for his LLC or corporation. He works anywhere from 40 to 80 hours a week, and rarely has a day off. He answers the phone and emails on weekends and late in the evening. He spends umpteen hours on a continuing basis on marketing, Internet technologies, his MLS service, and he spends a lot of money promoting his business to do what needs to be done to sell homes. This is the short list. A full list would be a dozen pages long. In short, a full time professional pours his life into his real estate business. He has to if he wants to be good and competitive.

So when a FSBO says, "I'll give you 2.5%," the agent is hearing, "I'll give you 2.5% if you will take all of your life's education and experience, all that you have invested in becoming a Realtor, all of your marketing, all that you have built to market real estate, both traditionally and on the Internet, the tens of thousands of dollars you have invested in your career, and bring me the buyer I couldn't find myself. Then I will pay you 2.5%, but I'm not going to sign any kind of contract with you now."

Most Realtors would consider it a little offensive or a little condescending. Regardless, I promise you Realtors will not bother showing a FSBO. Why would they? There is no agreement in writing that the seller will pay a commission. FSBOs have and often do rip off real estate agents after they do bring a buyer.

I know of an agent who brought a buyer and did a great job with all the paperwork and due diligence, and the FSBO refused to pay the agreed commission at the closing table, and he had an agreement in writing. What kind of seller does something like that? While many FSBOs have a bad taste in their mouths for agents, agents also have had bad experiences with less-than-forthright FSBOs.

In terms of reaching buyers, a FSBO doesn't have the massive database of potential buyers that hundreds of agents have. In most cases, a FSBO has no database of prospective buyers who are looking. In other words, a FSBO has no network to plug into. Top producing agents have a large network that they have built and pay for to generate buyer leads. It can take many years to build that kind of network. FSBOs have no network like that.

Some FSBOs are counting on a buyer seeing their *For Sale* sign at the end of their driveway. That's a long shot. What are the chances the right buyer will just happen to drive down your street and see your FSBO sign and call you? Out of 100 qualified buyers, I would guess one out of a hundred, maybe. Those are not good odds when it comes to marketing.

Not reaching qualified buyers may be the FSBO's greatest weakness and the biggest reason the vast majority of FSBOs fail to get sold. But as is often the case, failure is not the result of one issue, but the compounding of issues. You might survive one shortcoming, but two or three can sink the ship.

The second big challenge for a FSBO is pricing their home.

I did a study many years ago (the early 1980s) in Spokane, Washington while I was in law school and working in the summers as a real estate agent. My study compared the listing prices of FSBOs and similar homes listed by agents in the MLS. It was an informal study, but my conclusion was that FSBOs were overpriced by an average of $8,000 compared to MLS homes listed by agents. I bought my first home in that market for $40,000. It was a 1,100 square foot home with an additional 1,100 square foot unfinished basement, three bedrooms and two baths. So that gives you an idea of how overpriced FSBOs were in that market, because $8,000 of $40,000 is 20% of the price. Those were conservative estimates in that market.

Pricing a home takes more experience than almost anything else I will do to sell a home. I've written a book about how to figure out what the fair market value of a home is, and there's a lot more to it than most people, including agents, realize. It's not just a matter of looking at a couple of other similar sales. Comparable sales are an important part of the evaluation process, but even that takes a lot of experience.

I had an offer come in from another agent

outside my market on one of my listings. To justify her client's low-ball offer, she referred to one sale that was not even in this market, and she ignored the perfect comp that was just sold in this market, as well as several other reasonably close local comps. Her reasoning was so devoid of practical real estate knowledge, it was shocking to both me and my sellers.

I had another offer on another listing, and again that agent ignored the ideal comp that was one lot away from the subject property, and she tried to argue a very dissimilar property was a good comp at a much lower price. Either these agents are puffing with the hope they can steal the property at a low price for their clients, or they are incredibly ignorant about how to find and interpret good comps.

Using comps is just one of the methods I use to arrive at an accurate fair market value, but the point is that FSBOs rarely have access to all the subscription data on sales, let alone the experience to know how to find and use good comps to arrive at a reasonable listing price.

Pricing has always been a challenge for FSBOs. I hesitate to share this, but FSBOs have a strong tendency to overprice their homes. Since my study in the 1980s, I have seen this trend continue, and it is more pronounced today. I have seen FSBOs that are priced tens of thousands of dollars above fair market value.

The logical argument is often that they need to net a certain amount out of the sale, or they have more than that in it, or they will argue extensively that it is a very "special property." None of those arguments are persuasive to buyers. Buyers will correctly argue that fair market value is fair market value, and the home has no premium emotional value for them yet.

The third big challenge for a FSBO is negotiating the price and terms.

Few FSBOs are equipped to negotiate the price and terms with a buyer, whether that buyer is a novice or an experienced home owner. Negotiating the price of a home is not like negotiating at a garage sale, and while most FSBOs would readily concur, they still have little experience in the art of negotiating, which takes some of us a lifetime to master.

Make a mistake negotiating, and your buyer could be gone. Sometimes it doesn't take much to scare someone, and doing or saying the wrong thing can kill the transaction. It's not a matter of not being honest. Honesty and full disclosure are absolutely important. But many sellers have said the wrong things to buyers, or they have said it in a way that was offensive.

The vast majority of FSBOs do not have hundreds or thousands of real estate negotiations under their belt, and they don't have the experience of knowing what the parameters are for a negotiation like theirs.

Even if a FSBO did have the negotiating experience, it is rarely productive to negotiate on your own behalf. It is well known that an experienced third party negotiator can have more success.

<u>The fourth big challenge for a FSBO is handling the contracts and the legal requirements.</u>

Contracts have gotten more complicated, and a standard purchase and sale agreement with the appropriate addendums can easily be 15 to 20 pages. FSBOs do not have access to the latest legal contracts and addendums in most areas of the country. In my MLS there are over 100 different forms, and the right ones must be carefully selected for the terms of each transaction, depending on the county. The forms are part of the services offered by our MLS provider, and FSBOs won't have access to these documents.

Office supply stores no longer sell legal forms, at least not the fully updated set needed for the sale of real estate. Legal Zoom has legal forms, but trying to buy forms off the Internet for a local real estate transaction and comply with state and county laws could be a nightmare, if not impossible. Most FSBOs end up hiring an attorney, which is an added expense for a FSBO.

By the way, if you think you will hire an attorney to help you with your real estate transaction as a way to replace your Realtor, think again. Very few attorneys have a real estate background, and very few have any sales and negotiating background. I was a real estate attorney for 20 years, but I came from a real estate sales background before law school, and after I retired from law practice, I came back full circle to real estate brokerage. But I'm the only attorney I know of with this kind of real estate background.

In the real estate profession, attorneys are commonly thought of as "deal killers," because they don't have a negotiating or facilitating mindset. They just cannot seem to help themselves, and they will typically edit and change everything, offend the buyers, and kill the transaction. Any experienced agent will tell you this in a moment of blunt honesty. This is why agents wince when either the buyer or seller says they will have an attorney review the documents. An attorney can draft unambiguous contract language, but he doesn't know more than a good agent about facilitating the successful closing of a transaction—he knows less.

The fifth big challenge for a FSBO is handling the

buyer's due diligence.

A FSBO could be setting themselves up for a buyer misrepresentation lawsuit if they don't handle the state mandated disclosures properly, or if they don't handle all the due diligence and inspections precisely according to the law and the contract language. There are not only state mandated disclosures, there are Federally mandated forms, and there are legally required contract addendums. In some cases the exact language must be used to comply with the law. Then there are deadlines and timelines that must be complied with contractually.

I have seen FSBOs do some research, buy or borrow some forms, and think they are smart by saving a commission, only to find themselves in a big legal mess. If a seller makes a mistake and a buyer gets hurt, you can bet the buyer will sue. Attorney's fees alone in a lawsuit can run $20,000 to $40,000 in a real estate case. If you lose, there goes a big part of your equity, not to mention one to two years of litigation. When you think the real estate commission might have only been $6,000 to $10,000, is it really worth all the risk?

The FSBO Disadvantages for the Buyer

Apart from the challenges for a FSBO in marketing and connecting with the right buyer, and then handling all the negotiations and contracts and due diligence, and getting all the way to closing despite inspectors and underwriters, there are challenges for buyers of FSBOs, too.

These challenges for buyers parallel the FSBO's challenges, but they are examined from a buyer's perspective with more detail that is relevant for sellers to understand.

The first big challenge for a buyer is finding the FSBO.

Buyers are using online MLS sites built and paid for by real estate brokers who also have to pay for what is called an IDX data feed from the MLS database that feeds all the data into their public MLS sites. These sites are where buyers are looking, and FSBOs do not show up here.

Even for the buyers who use Zillow or Trulia, those IDX data feeds are also coming from the local MLS, so if a FSBO is not listed by an agent and put in the local MLS, it doesn't show up as a listing for sale in Zillow or Trulia. It will still show up as all properties do in those services, because those services are now including every home in America, whether it is listed or not. But that is no help to buyers, because the selling information and price will not be there. Sometimes you can't tell if a home on Zillow or Trulia is for sale, or if it is just part of the massive database of real estate information on every home in America. Buyers are starting to learn that Zillow is full of defective information on properties, and they are looking for accurate local MLS sites.

Buyers are searching in a number of ways using different sites, and one of the ways they search is by using a search engine. To be found in the search engines, one must have high search engine ranking, and that happens through good organic search engine optimization (SEO). FSBOs lose out here, too. It takes years and a lot of expertise to build high search engine ranking for listings and real estate information, and FSBOs do not have that. Even the FSBO sites where they can pay to post their property do not have good ranking, so buyers simply don't find those homes when they are searching. You can be on the Internet and still be invisible, and that's what is happening with FSBOs.

The point is that if buyers cannot easily find a home for sale, they will never see it. FSBOs suffer from being invisible to buyers.

The second big challenge for a buyer is knowing how to determine fair market value.

Buyers are skeptical of FSBOs and their prices, especially if they are from outside the area. They wonder how the FSBO came up with the listing price, and they would like comps. Apart from the fact that a buyer is not going to trust a FSBO's promise that the price is fair market value (FMV), neither the FSBO nor the buyer have access to the local MLS data on comparable sales. This is no small dilemma. How do you compare sales if you can't search the database of similar properties that have sold in the past few months? The public county auditor's files are not programmed to search for the purpose of preparing a comparative market analysis (CMA). If a FSBO cannot satisfy a buyer on price, this could be the end of the negotiations. Imagine how awkward that discussion on price might go.

<u>The third big challenge for a buyer is negotiating the price and terms.</u>

What if one of parties is experienced in negotiating, but the other is not? That could be a one-sided disaster. If you're a seller, and you're hoping a buyer will pay more than your home is worth, don't hold your breath. Buyers are smart these days. They are doing a lot of research on homes on the Internet long before they start walking through homes. If they feel they got fooled, you can quickly become a defendant in an expensive lawsuit. And did you know a buyer can walk away from the transaction one minute before signing the closing papers? Imagine starting all over. What a nightmare that would be, and it does happen.

Granted, they could lose their earnest money, but that won't make you whole.

What if both buyer and seller are experts in negotiating? That is extremely unlikely, but if they are, they still don't have access to all the comps in the MLS, so they are going to have trouble figuring out what the true FMV is. If you don't start with FMV, it's hard to negotiate from a solid base. They could hire an appraiser, but three appraisers will come up with three different numbers.

By the way, if both buyer and seller are expert negotiators from prior careers, the odds of them reaching an agreement are almost nil. They are both trained to negotiate hard and to walk away before losing, so they will almost certainly kill the negotiations after days and sometimes weeks of games. Alphas don't take losing very well.

<u>The fourth big challenge for a buyer is handling the contracts and the legal requirements.</u>

Buyers are favored now in the law, meaning that consumer protection has swung in favor of buyers and against sellers. In a standard Purchase & Sale Agreement and the standard addendums, a buyer has several ways to terminate the transaction and get his earnest money back, but a seller does not have those options. In other words, the state of contract law now is that buyers can walk away, but sellers cannot. And a seller who does not cross every "T" and dot every "I" with all the documents, processes, and timelines will find himself in an indefensible position since the law defaults to favor buyers.

In this era of complicated contracts and legal liabilities, transactions hang by a hair until closing, and that's assuming you do everything exactly right. Do one thing wrong, phrase something slightly incorrect in a financing addendum or in an inspection response form, check the wrong box (or not), and the buyer's loan underwriter will disqualify the loan. There are a thousand traps for the unwary FSBO and their buyer.

<u>The fifth big challenge for a buyer is working through the due diligence.</u>

There are a number of inspections and numerous issues that must be checked out during the pending of the contract and prior to the deadlines in the contracts. All of these inspections must be done right, and the buyer must be satisfied, and his lender must be satisfied. If a problem or a potential problem comes up as the result of one of the inspections, there are specific legal requirements and good and bad ways to handle it. Agents learn all these things from a lot of education and from years in the real estate school of hard knocks. A buyer of a FSBO takes great risk trying to learn by himself in the middle of his own transaction.

Conclusion

I know there will be a FSBO who reads this chapter and insists that I am biased because I am a real estate broker. I understand that kind of thinking, but it is precisely because I have so much experience in real estate that I could write this chapter. Every single word and sentence in this chapter was carefully chosen and edited many times to be certain of its accuracy. I stand by my arguments in this chapter.

Not in 100 years would I try to market my own home as a FSBO if I were the average homeowner without my experience. Don't do it. There is a very high probability you will eventually say to yourself through clenched teeth, "We've wasted a year and a lot of money and it's been stressful. And we have nothing to show for it, except more gray hair."

---

[1] Secret No. 12. FSBOs have a huge disadvantage in pricing and negotiating. It is such a disadvantage that few FSBOs ever get their homes sold themselves. Over 85% end up listing, and most of the remaining 15% give up on trying to sell at all.

[2] Secret No. 13. The biggest challenge for FSBOs is connecting with qualified buyers. Few FSBOs have any kind of powerful marketing system in place for their homes.

Bonus Chapters

Chapter 8
26-Point Interview Checklist

What questions should a home seller ask a listing agent in an interview? The majority of home sellers don't know some of the most relevant questions they need to ask listing agents. Since the answers you get are only as good as the questions you ask, your interview questions are extremely important.

These 26 questions make excellent interview questions for your prospective real estate agent. The answers your agent gives you to these questions will tell you so much about your agent and what he can do for you. But don't let him get away with a simple "yes" or "no" to these questions. They require narrative answers, and an experienced agent has good answers for all of them. Obviously, your discernment meter must be on and fully functional.

By the time you are done interviewing your prospective agent, you will have a pretty good idea not only what his knowledge and experience levels are, but also what his personality is like. Personality is very important in sales.

Do not expect your agent to pass your interview with a perfect score. While the answers can vary and still be good, good agents' responses will have a common thread of competence, professionalism, and honesty that you should pick up on.

There are more questions that could be asked, and you may feel these 26 questions are too much, but every single question is supported by years of experience. In other words, there are a lot of legitimate reasons for every single question.

After each question I've included a short commentary that explains the importance and value of the question and answer.

1. How many years have you been in real estate sales?

It takes 10 years to become an expert in any field, but that's not a guarantee an agent will be an expert. It depends on whether she has been teachable and pursuing her career to become the best real estate professional she can become. In this business an agent must take learning seriously, and every day is another day to learn something new and get better and better. We learn in classes, but more importantly we learn in the school of hard knocks and from every transaction.

You would think every agent would be eager more, and become a better professional with experience. Alas, it is not so. At a minimum require 10 years of full time experience. Beginners have to learn by trial and error with some home sellers, just not you.

2. Are you a full time agent or a part time agent?

It might be nice to be a part time agent and pop a commission now and then, but you want a full time professional who takes his career seriously. Part time agents know less, have less experience, and have other priorities. You wouldn't hire a part time doctor. Why hire a part time agent?

3. Tell me about traditional marketing in real estate and what you do that is different?

This may be the most important question you ask. His answer will reveal a lot about his knowledge of marketing. A real estate agent is in the business of marketing, so clearly he should be an expert in marketing. This means he should be able to talk all about marketing, various media, how marketing has evolved in the real estate industry, and he should be able to talk about the statistics of various advertising approaches. Of course, you don't have hours for him to go on and on, which means he needs to be good at summarizing and hitting the main points quickly. And you need to discern the difference between B.S. and truth.

He should be able to talk about print advertising, radio, mailings, open houses, and the many online advertising options. He should know the effectiveness of each and be able to compare metrics and what is most effective today. Marketing a home effectively today is absolutely critical to connecting with the most qualified buyers, and it is the qualified buyer who will pay the highest price for your home.

Poor marketing that doesn't connect with the most qualified buyers, but merely drags the bottom for any buyer will mean getting low offers and being forced to sell to buyers who are incapable or unwilling to pay fair market value for your home. You need an agent who knows and practices good marketing.

4. Tell me about Internet marketing in real estate?

This is an extension of the last question, but it is absolutely critical that your agent understands how to use technology and the Internet. Today a successful agent must also become an expert in Internet marketing. If she is not, move on. This is that important. Why? Over 95% of all buyers start their searching online! What does that tell you?

If you know nothing about Internet marketing

yourself, you will be at a disadvantage in understanding the agent's answer, but if you have a high level of discernment, you should be able to discern insight and knowledge from a shallow answer. Of course, you should ask her about her own Internet marketing system. Does she have one? How is it working out for her?

5. How many of your own listings did you sell to buyers yourself in the past 12 months? In other words, in how many of your closings did you act as a dual agent?

This is important. Do not ask, "How many homes did you sell in the past 12 months?" That's a wide open question with room for all kinds of exaggeration. Let me explain.

Many agents simply list, list, and list, and other agents sell those listings. What is more impressive, an agent who lists a lot of properties that other agents sell, or the agents who sell most of the listings? Now perhaps you can understand the importance of this fifth question.

Be sure to clarify with the agents you interview, that you want to know how many homes they listed, how many homes they listed that were sold by other agents, and how many homes they listed and sold themselves? Do not let them blur it all together to make themselves sound better than they really are. All you want is a true picture of their success. That's all.

6. How many homes (that were not your listings) have you closed as a buyer's agent over the past 12 months? A buyer's agent is a selling agent when he represents a buyer and sells a home he did not list. In the MLS the agent who sells a home is the selling agent, which is different than the "seller's agent".

It doesn't matter if your prospective agent is number 1 or 2 or 3 or 20 in the MLS statistics. What matters is that he is a top producer in this new world of marketing. But this is not the only important credential. An agent can be a top producer and not satisfy many of the other important criteria.

7. How many listings do you have now? Tell me about some of them.

The real reason for this question is to see if she is listing nice properties like yours. The kind of properties that an agent lists says a lot about the buyers she connects with. If your home is a $350,000 modern craftsman, and she lists a lot of foreclosures and mobile homes, is she the right agent to list your home? Probably not.

There is a small red flag that is raised when an agent does have a lot of listings and uses that as an argument that you should list with her. What if she is the kind of agent who lists, lists, and lists, and that is her total focus? What if she doesn't really have a great marketing system to buyers, and what if she is the kind of agent who throws listings in the MLS and waits for other agents to sell those properties?

A great agent might have a few listings or a lot of listings, and a poor agent might have a few listings or a lot of listings. Discernment is the key here. This is why you need to ask a number of questions and do your due diligence on each agent.

8. Describe the profile of your ideal clients.

You want an agent who works with clients like yourself. If you are selling an $800,000 home, you do not want an agent who specializes in foreclosures under $150,000. He won't be connecting with buyers for homes like yours. Most people don't think about this, but this is very important.

Ask about the buyers that he regularly works with. His marketing will attract buyers with a certain profile. What is that profile? Does that profile describe someone who buys homes like yours in that price range? You can't ask him that directly, because he will give you the answer you want to hear.

9. What are your values and what role do

they play in your business model?[1]

This is where a narrative answer will reveal a lot about your agent. Honesty and integrity are absolutely critical. Never put yourself in the position of depending on an agent who is not honest to the core.

10. Is there one MLS in this market or two? If there are two, are you a member of both? If not, why not?

In my little market of Sequim, Washington, there are two MLSs. A home seller needs to get exposed to as many agents and as many of those agents' buyers as possible. That means promoting the listing in both the NWMLS (Northwest MLS) and in the OLS MLS (Olympic Listing Service).

11. Tell me how you market listings? What do you do that is traditional, and what do you do that uses technology and the Internet? I would like to know how you intend to market my home on the Internet.

This and the next question are the core of what a successful real estate agent does in this new world of marketing. Turn on your discernment meter and listen carefully. If you have to, take notes so you can find out later from someone who is knowledgeable if the answers are credible. How much due diligence you decide to put into the interview and research phase of hiring an agent is up to you, but if I had tens of thousands of dollars at stake, I would do a lot of research until I was completely satisfied.

12. How do you connect with buyers? What kind of marketing do you use to reach qualified buyers, and how do you filter out the unqualified?

This is one of the keys to success for an agent today. Some agents only list, and they don't have a powerful marketing system in place. But there are agents who not only know how to list and market those listings, they also know how to market successfully to qualified buyers and are closing transactions as a result.

13. What is your experience with negotiating? How do you negotiate for your clients?

Negotiating the price and negotiating the terms is not for inexperienced agents. It's your money, so be certain you hire the best negotiator. Read more about negotiating by searching SequimRealEstateNews.com for the word "negotiating." You will find at least a dozen articles discussing various aspects of effective negotiating.

14. What is your experience level with contracts and addendums and drafting

unique language for special situations?[2]

This might seem like a small matter compared to the other questions, but as they say, "The devil is in the details." You need an agent who can cross all the "Ts" and dot all the "Is" for your sake on every aspect of your transaction. Your agent docs not have to have the experience of a lawyer like I do, but they should be very good at using the English language unambiguously and articulating exactly what any unique terms are in your transaction so there will be absolutely no confusion or misunderstanding by anyone involved.

I don't want to beat this subject up too much, but I cannot over emphasize how important it is. Usually people find out after the fact when they are in a dispute, because their agent didn't complete the legal documents correctly.

I'll share one real life example. I received an offer on one of my listings from an agent outside of my market. The offer was not cleanly typed. All the blanks were completed with handwritten information, but much of it was not legible. The document was apparently scanned, but a lot of the print was too light to read, and her scanner was apparently not set to the right size page, so everything was smaller than normal.

If you think all that is unbelievable, wait because there's more. There were options that were not checked but should have been. There were pages missing. There was an entire addendum missing. Some of the pages were upside down. In all my years in real estate, this is one of the worse offers I have ever seen. On top of that, the offering price was ridiculously and unreasonably low. I'm not making this up. They say that, "truth is stranger than fiction," and I think that's true. I really did wonder if her clients had any idea what a terrible job their agent did on that offer.

15. How good are you at communicating in writing, and I mean in letters, emails, and other written communications with everyone you deal with?[3]

Outstanding written communication skills should be one of your minimum qualifications for any agent. If your agent cannot communicate clearly in writing to you and to everyone else who will be involved in your real estate transaction, you will have problems. Every critical communication in real estate happens in written form, whether that is in a contract, an amendment to the contract, an email or a letter. Verbal communications are not binding in real estate, but written communications are.

This is huge, because being able to articulate a thought or a term or a condition unambiguously is not a common skill. As a lawyer I edited hundreds of real estate clauses that were so full of holes you could drive a Mac truck through them. The last thing you want in your sale is a gigantic loophole that gives the buyer an unfair advantage over how and when you close.

How you qualify an agent on this skill is up to you, but you could email with them on some specific questions and see how clearly and thoroughly they respond. You could read some of their sales narratives on listings, but some listing agents hire someone else to write that for them. Better yet, you should read some of their articles on their real estate blog. Their articles should be directed to buyers, and they should be informative, well written and interesting. If their writing is poor and not persuasive, that's a bad sign. A major part of what we do in marketing and sales involves clear and persuasive writing.

16. How do you help your clients through all the critical steps between mutual acceptance and closing?

There are many tasks that need to be done, and someone who knows all the steps and all the hurdles needs to step up and be the adult who supervises everyone else involved. Who better than your agent? If not him, then who?

Your agent should work by your side until closing, and be willing to help you work through every detail all the way to closing.

17. Do you help your clients understand the preliminary title report? How do you do that?

This is important, because the title report and the attached documents will reveal all the restrictions on the property, the easements, and any recorded mortgages, liens, and encumbrances. You should not have to hire an attorney for this. And your agent doesn't have to be an attorney to acquire this kind of knowledge after 10 years in the business.

If the title company needs something done to make the property insurable or to clear something off the title, your agent may not have the expertise to know exactly how to do it, and he is not responsible for drafting legal documents, but he certainly should understand the issues and coordinate a resolution with the professionals you may need to hire.

I listed a home, and when we had it sold, the title company told us there was an easement that was defective. A surveyor had done the survey, and then he practiced law without a license and drafted an easement that he had no business drafting. It was legally insufficient, so I met with an attorney on behalf of my seller and told him what we needed. He drafted it, and

I tracked down the parties who needed to sign it. We got it done. If I didn't know how to do that, the transaction might not have closed since the title would not have been insurable.

18. Do you help buyers understand the CC&Rs?

This is a relevant question, because buyers need to understand what they can and cannot do on their property. What if you cannot park your boat or your motor home on your property? What if there is a view easement that effects your property? What if a buyer wants to have a horse? If a buyer cannot get a straight answer, he may walk away from your property without ever making an offer.

19. Do you help your clients with home inspections, well inspections, and septic inspections?

I had a client tell me his last sale was with an agent who would not help him at all with the inspections that needed to be done. She drafted the offer and they had mutual acceptance, but when he ask her if she would help him schedule the inspections, she told him curtly, "I don't do that. My job is done." I was absolutely shocked when I heard that. So was her client.

Will your agent schedule inspections and attend

them? If not your agent, then who? These are critically important inspections. A good agent will go above and beyond to make sure you are taken care of all the way to closing and beyond. Actually, a professional will consider it part of the customer service he gives every single client.

20. Tell me about your customer service and how you communicate with your clients. What kind of CRM (customer relationship management software) do you use, and tell me how it will help you sell my home.[4]

The biggest complaint today across the country is, "my agent put my listing in the MLS and then I never heard from him again," or words to that effect. Listing agents talk big at listing presentations, but living up to all the hype is hard. Promises, promises, promises. Agents make them all the time. Talk is cheap, but the agent who actually does what he says he will do is worth his weight in gold.

The other reason how your listing agent communicates is important is because he will be communicating with many buyers and prospective buyers, and being an effective communicator is everything. Follow up is also important, and that's an important part of any CRM system.

21. What advantage do you offer me that

no other agent can offer?

This is a narrative opportunity for an agent to sell himself. If he can't sell himself persuasively to you, don't expect him to be good at selling real estate. The other questions you ask him about his real estate knowledge and marketing have already been answered. What you're looking for here is confidence with humility, and a winning personality that is genuinely transparent. Your listing agent should be likable. Very likeable. Otherwise, how is he going to sell your home and your neighborhood and your town?

You should also pick up a sense of passion for the area and for working with his clients. Your agent doesn't just sell your home, he sells your area, your town, your county, and the benefits of living in your area. Then he sells your home. All of these things happen in large part because of his passion for what he does and the wonderful relationships he is able to build with clients, especially buyers. That's why personality is so important.

22. Tell me about your public MLS site and your real estate blog.

Your agent should have a large and effective Internet presence. Nearly every buyer is using the Internet, and that's where 95% of buyers start their home search. Your agent should have an excellent MLS site and a very good and content rich real estate blog.

Obviously, good content is king. The author must have depth of knowledge about the real estate business. As a marketing tool, real estate articles should address specific concerns that buyers have, and should do that with credibility.

But there is more to attracting buyers than great content alone. Did you know there is a psychology of colors? The wrong colors can push buyers away at the subconscious level. A site must also be intuitively navigable so that information and links will be where buyers expect them to be based on their prior experiences and habits on the Internet.

The articles need to speak to buyers based on their needs, and videos should connect with buyers' visual needs for information. There must not only be solid information, precisely the kind of information that they are searching for, but the sites must also connect with buyers on an emotional level. Facts alone do not sell.

The sites also need to be findable, meaning that under the hood of a beautiful blog or website, there must be powerful SEO (search engine optimization) so that buyers will find the sites. If this is not done, the sites will never be indexed and ranked high enough for buyers to ever find them.

You can see why I say there is so much more to effectively marketing real estate to qualified buyers today than in past years. One needs real estate knowledge, real estate experience, sales experience, marketing knowledge, and technological know-how to make it all happen. And while many agents would be unhappy to hear this, outstanding marketing of a home today requires good writing skills.

For examples of a real estate blog and an MLS site that are setting the standard in the State of Washington, see:

SequimRealEstateNews.com

Sequim-Homes.com

23. Can I see some testimonies of past clients, including at least one listing client, at least one client you represented as a buyer's agent, and a client you represented as a dual agent?

What past clients say will tell you volumes. It would be great if you could call a past client on the phone, but most clients won't want to keep getting phone calls from strangers asking for testimonies. An agent should have a collection of great testimonies for you. They may be posted on his blog. Apart from these questions, you should do your own independent research online. You can find out all about a real estate agent if you know how to search online.

24. What is your commission, and do you charge me anything to list with you?

Don't get hung up on whether the commission is 5% or 6% for homes.[5] That is the least of your concerns. A good listing agent will market your home effectively to connect with the most qualified buyers, hence getting the highest possible price from the best offers. In addition, a good listing agent is a master negotiator. A listing agent who is not experienced in these two areas can cost you far more than the entire commission.

Don't forget that the total commission is split equally between your listing agent and the selling agent, so if the total commission is 6%, your listing agent will earn 3% if another agent sells your property. Some brokers will agree to reduce the commission if they act as a dual agent.

Beware that some agents have found another way to increase their income by charging you to list with them. There is nothing illegal or unethical about doing that, but when a listing agent charges her clients $1,000 to $3,000 plus a commission, you'd better look hard at that opportunity. They may also tell you they will credit you that up front fee at closing. Right. And if they don't close, you don't get it back.

Another trick agents may use to get money from you up front is to tell you the money is needed to advance costs, like the cost of photographs by a professional, or certain Internet subscription fees to promote your property. Don't buy any of those pitches. Why do you think you are going to pay a huge commission? It is to cover all the costs of marketing your property plus put a profit in your agent's pocket. That's how it works, and that's how it has worked for decades. I don't charge my clients up front, and neither do other outstanding top producers around the country.

If an agent thinks she is so good, why would she have to charge you something up front? Do you think she knows she may not sell your home?

And don't buy the argument that, "I'm busy and the best listing agent on the planet, and if you want to list with me, you have to pay me up front." The best agents earn good commissions, because they sell homes. They don't need to get money out of you up front.

Remember, for some it is all about listings, listings, and more listings. Enough said.

25. Tell me how you use photography to sell my home. What is your experience with photography? What kind of camera equipment do you have, and what photo editing software do you use? (The same question should be asked about videos.)

I recommend you read Chapter 10, How Important Are Photographs? A listing agent must have the requisite photographic equipment, the knowledge and experience, and good editing software.

In Chapter 10 I wrote, "When it comes to looking at homes online, everyone is visual. One quick glance of an ugly home, and you're gone, right? And it doesn't take 10 seconds to dump that home to look at others. According to Internet navigation experts, Internet shoppers will only give you three to five seconds, and they're gone. So what captures and keeps their attention first? Good photos."

I think it would be a good idea to see some of an agent's previous MLS photos. Wouldn't that tell you a lot? That alone would be worth a thousand words.

26. The Non-Quantifiables

This is the subjective part of the analysis, and you must do it yourself after you have interviewed your prospective listing agent(s). She cannot answer this question for you. This involves what I call the "non-quantifiables." These are the attributes or characteristics of an agent that cannot be quantified in any way, but are extremely important. What am I talking about?

Nearly every licensed profession has tests that must be passed in order to get licensed. That is true of real estate agents, but it is also true of lawyers, mortgage brokers, appraisers, insurance agents, and so many other professionals. We all know this, but here's the question. Does passing a written test and paying a fee to get a license prove an individual is qualified in all respects? Of course not. It doesn't even guarantee that con artists or incompetents will be filtered out.

I estimate that the questions on a real estate licensing exam cover less than $1/100^{th}$ of 1% of what a knowledgeable agent has learned over 10 to 30 years in the business. Even then, we are only talking about factual knowledge, contract language, Federal prohibitions on advertising, state brokerage law, and so on.

In real estate, an agent can pass the test and get licensed by jumping through the hoops. The bar is not very high. I'm not suggesting that the test should be harder or that other bureaucratic hurdles should be raised before an agent is issued a license. There are some who argue that the barriers to entry should be higher, but they are wrong, and here's why.

You cannot legislate honesty, integrity, good character, hard work, loyalty, professionalism, commitment, creativity, teachability, humility, and so on. No amount of testing will create these things, and yet these are more important than all the rest of the credentials upon which the written tests are based. The most important attributes in your listing agent are the non-quantifiables!

Even if you could quantify these subjective attributes in a written test, there are those who would learn the acceptable answers, and they would pass the test. But they still would not possess those qualities.

This will be your most important task--identifying an agent who passes the other questions to your satisfaction, and also passes your standards on these non-quantifiables. It is these non-quantifiables that make a good agent a great agent.

---

[1] Secret No. 14. Values are important. Honesty, integrity, hard work, loyalty, perseverance, competence, and professionalism are so important, yet most home sellers don't examine their listing agent on these issues.

[2] Secret No. 15. Solid real estate knowledge and experience are extremely important, yet most home sellers don't test their prospective listing agents on knowledge and experience.

[3] Secret No. 16. Communication skills are a vital part of an agent's

work, and important in succeeding to sell your home for the highest price. These skills include more than just verbal skills. They include writing and drafting contract language, advertisements, MLS narratives, email communicatoins, and telephone conversations.

[4] Secret No. 17. Customer service is sorely lacking in the real estate profession. Clarify what kind of customer service your listing agent will provide prior to listing. Did you get that in writing?

[5] The larger the commission, the more agents are going to try to sell your home. That's no small thing. At 6%, the selling agent representing a buyer would earn 3%. That is a big motivator for an agent to sell your home.

Chapter 9
Never Let an Offer Die

Never Let An Offer Die is one of my rules as a real estate broker. Whether I am making an offer on behalf of a buyer, or receiving an offer from another real estate agent on a listing, I never let an offer die. This is incredibly important for buyers and sellers, and let me explain exactly why.

·I represented a buyer who asked me to draft an offer on a nice home. I did, and I submitted the offer to the listing agent. When I submit an offer, I scan it and email it to the listing agent, and then I call the listing agent immediately to let him or her know it is in their inbox. After three days of no news and no response from the listing agent, both my client and I were getting impatient. Finally, on the 3rd day the listing agent emailed me to let me know that the sellers chose on the first day not to respond to the offer at all.

This is a text book example of how not to handle an offer on the seller's end. It was not very courteous of the listing agent to delay like that, but that's not my primary concern here. Had the seller and their agent applied the simple rule, *Never Let An Offer Die*, there would have been a counteroffer, and we would have reached an agreement.

How do I know we would have reached an agreement? Because my client and I applied the rule, *Never Let An Offer Die*, and we re-submitted the offer and forced the seller and their agent to respond until we finally did reach mutual acceptance. Had we not applied this rule, the seller would not have sold their home to this buyer, and who knows when they would have sold their home.

I drafted and submitted another offer for a client from Texas. The listing agent did not acknowledge receipt of the offer, and did not respond to repeated phone calls and emails. Weeks went by. Nothing.

Finally I reached the listing agent on the phone, and we had a conversation about the property and whether the seller would respond. I was reassured that the seller would respond. I drafted a new offer and submitted that to the same agent on the same house. Nothing.

As a buyer's agent, I was prohibited from contacting the seller directly. [Some MLSs and associations have rules that address this problem now.]

My client was not be able to buy that house, although I am certain the seller wanted to sell. Again, if the rule, *Never Let An Offer Die*, had been applied by the listing agent, we might have closed that transaction.

I drafted and submitted an offer on a listing that was overpriced (at just under $600,000), and the listing agent told me that his client was not even going to respond. It was a short conversation, because he then said, "Goodbye." No counteroffer. Nothing. I watched that listing, and the listing expired after more than 500 days with the price finally down to what my client's offer was ($400,000).

I understand if sellers don't know about my rule, *Never Let An Offer Die*, but real estate agents should know and practice this rule for the benefit of their own clients. Of course, they would also earn a commission they might not otherwise earn if they practiced the rule.

The logic of the rule becomes apparent when you think about what it takes to get one interested and qualified buyer who wants to make an offer on a home in the worst real estate recession I've seen in over three decades in the business. Good marketing reaches large numbers of potential buyers, and to some extent, like sales in any industry, it's a numbers game.

For every one buyer who closes on a transaction, I have emailed and talked to hundreds on the phone. To connect with those hundreds, I have connected with thousands through articles, videos, and an extensive marketing system. To connect with thousands I have literally had millions read my real estate articles, and all of that filters down through what salesmen often call the sales funnel and ultimately to a closing. So getting that one client that actually closes on a transaction is the culmination of an awful lot of hard work, not to mention a lot of money and a lot of time over a period of years.

Walking away from that one buyer who may come along once in six months would be absolutely crazy or totally reckless. In this market, and frankly in any market, it would be crazy if you had a serious buyer and serious seller not making an effort to reach mutual acceptance. A buyer and seller should exhaust all efforts to reach an agreement before they walk away from the negotiating table.

If you had a car advertised for sale for $4,000 on Craigslist, and someone called you and asked you if you would consider $3,750, would you hang up on them? Of course not. If you were selling a home listed for $400,000, and someone offered $375,000, would you not even respond to the offer? You can see why I place so much emphasis on this rule, *Never Let an Offer Die.*

In cases where an agent on the other end of a transaction gave up quickly and made no apparent attempt to keep the negotiations going, I have had clients who shook their heads and ask, "why would an agent not make every effort to keep the negotiations going when he doesn't earn a commission unless it closes?"

Not all questions about real estate can be answered objectively. So long as human beings are less than perfect, we will have problems on this planet. Real estate agents are human beings, and that means their behavior will run the gamut of human behavior. You didn't think they were all perfect, did you?

Practicing this rule, *Never Let An Offer Die,* does not guarantee that you will reach mutual acceptance, but it does substantially increase the chances of closing the deal. It's a simple rule, but it is one of the most powerful and effective negotiating rules on the table.

Chapter 10
How Important Are Photographs?

When it comes to looking at homes online, everyone is visual. One quick glance of an ugly home, and you're gone, right? And it doesn't take 10 seconds to dump that home to look at others. According to Internet navigation experts, Internet shoppers will only give you three to five seconds, and if they don't like what they see, they're gone. So what captures and keeps their attention first? Good photos.

Here's the problem in a nutshell. Buyer's call and email me all the time asking me questions like these about many MLS listings.[1]

Questions Buyers Ask All The Time

"Is there no master bedroom? There are no photos."

"There isn't a photo of the master bathroom. Is there a master bathroom, and how big is it?"

"What's behind the house. There's a photo of

the front yard, but nothing out back."

"What does the inside of the shop look like? Is it finished? Is there a concrete floor? There isn't a photo of the inside of the shop."

But wait the questions get better. I get questions like these.

"There is only one photo from the end of the driveway. Aren't there any more photos?"

"There are only three photos, and none of the interior. Two of the photos are of a shed outside. What's going on?"

"There's a close up water view, but on Google the house is several miles from the shoreline. Is that photo for real or was it taken with a powerful telephoto?"

"I can't figure out the floor plan from the six photos that are in the MLS. Can you help me?"

"What does the general neighborhood look like? The photos are all interior shots with only one of the front of the house."

Three Reasons Why Buyers Are Frustrated With MLS Photos

I believe there are three main reasons buyers get frustrated with MLS photos. This is my opinion based on examining thousands of listings over a period of more than two decades, and based on talking to hundreds of clients on this subject. This is not a scientific or statistically tested conclusion, but it does come with a lot of research and specific analysis on this issue.

My conservative conclusion is that more than 50% of all MLS listings suffer from one or more of the following three serious defects:[2]

1. Not Enough Photos

2. The Wrong Photos

3. Poor Photos

I want to explain each of these, so you will know what I am talking about, and you'll be able to do some of your own analysis if you choose.[3]

Keep in mind what buyers expect to find when they look at homes online. Buyers want to be able to get a true vignette of what a home and the property look like. The best visual presentation of a listing in the MLS is one which most accurately helps a buyer get an honest feel for what the property actually looks and feels like, not only the interior, but the exterior and around the house.

Buyers don't just buy a living room and kitchen. They buy the entire home and property, the neighborhood and the community. If photos don't sell a home well, then the MLS listing falls short and leaves them wondering. If several listings leave a buyer wondering, but two other listings have wonderful photos that give that buyer a complete explanation of the home, which homes do you think they will put on their favorites list, and which ones do you think they may ignore and never look at?

Not Enough Photos

One of the most common problems with MLS listings is that they don't have enough photos. Each local MLS service has it's own programming requirements for how many photos can be uploaded to the MLS and what size and quality of photos should be uploaded. Unfortunately, there is no nationwide standard, so an agent must master the technical requirements of uploading photos in the MLS for her own listings.

If a local MLS allows a maximum of 15 or even up to 20 photos of a home, why would anyone shoot less than the maximum allowed? I can't get inside other agents' heads, but I can tell you what buyers are asking about this, and what buyers are thinking is everything.

Buyers say things like, "Well, if they don't want us to see that part of the house, there must be something wrong. Scratch it off the list," or "That's so strange they wouldn't have a photo of the living room or the laundry room or the master shower. They must want to hide something."

Here's something buyers shake their heads over all the time. They rhetorically ask, "Why would a listing agent try to hide or misrepresent what a house really looks like? Does he think he can trick us into buying it? Does he think we won't notice that the water view photo in the MLS does not match the actual view? When we get here and find out, we only get ticked off, and would never hire that listing agent to be our buyer's agent." Burning buyers is not a good method for marketing any home.

Buyers want to get a good feel for a home and the whole setting, so it takes a lot more than 13 or 17 or 20 photos to do that, but every MLS limits the number of photos an agent can upload. We have to work within the limitations of our MLS. But a good marketing agent will do much more than just rely on MLS photos to market a property.

As I have looked at MLS listings, I am surprised at how many listings are missing photos. A large percentage of listings have less than the maximum allowable photos, and I have been a bit shocked to find listings with only one, two, or three photos!

The challenge a good listing agent has is not uploading the maximum number of photos—it's figuring out which photos will make the best presentation possible out of a much larger number of photos that were taken.

On a typical photo shoot I will take 30 to 40 photos of the interior and exterior of a home as well as the outdoor views. In some cases, I take over 100 photos. You can only edit good photos, and if you don't have enough good photos to edit back at the computer, you're in trouble.

Remember, this is all about buyers. It's not about what your eyes expect, because you already know your property inside out. It's not about what your agent thinks is important. It's about what buyers know is important, and it is the eyes of buyers we are trying to reach and impress.

The Wrong Photos

It's one thing to fill the MLS listing with all the photos possible, and it's quite another to give buyers the kind of quality photos they need to get an accurate depiction of your property. It does no good to have a bunch of wrong photos.

There are two extremely important aspects to the right photos. First, they must be the precise photos buyers want and expect to see, and they must be taken with the right perspective. This means the right rooms, the right exterior shots, the right views around the property, and the right angles.

This takes a photographic eye. If I may defend listing agents for a second, not all listing agents are trained photographers. In fact, very few are. Few have an eye for photography at this professional level. That's not much of a defense I know, but the point is listing agents don't generally know how to take the right photos with the right perspectives. That's not really a legitimate excuse, because a listing agent is selling his photography, too. What is the single most important aspect of marketing a home? Great photos. At least that's where it starts.

But it's not just about the knowledge of how to take good photos. It's also about the necessary equipment. A cheap camera simply won't be capable of taking great photos. It is limited in how fast the digital chip is, meaning it is limited by how much light can be captured to record a clear image.

Street cameras have a limited range when it comes to lighting and lenses. The speed of a lens is important, which again goes to how much natural light can be captured. If flash or lamps are required, we still are trying to get a natural look.

A wide angle lens is essential, but too wide will create distortion. We've all seen photos taken with an extreme wide angle lens causing the outer edges of the image to curve unnaturally. That doesn't look good in an MLS photo. Sometimes it is appropriate to use a telephoto lens, but just like a wide angle lens, you can get an image that does not accurately depict a property or the view.

Do you know what really ticks off buyers all the time? Dishonest photography. Here's an example. A buyer is sitting in Santa Barbara, California looking online at homes far away where they want to retire. They find one with spectacular water views, and they are excited. They put the home at the top of their short list of favorites, and they tell their buyer's agent they want to see that home first.

Alas, when they stand on the deck of that home with the incredible water view photo, they are very disappointed. The listing agent who took the photo used a super telephoto lens, and the water view actually is way off in the distance. The home is at least ten miles from the water.

The buyers are not just disappointed, they are asking what is wrong with that listing agent. A number of buyers have asked me a question like, "Why would he misrepresent the home and the view like this? Does he think he can fool us into buying it? Unbelievable!" That's what buyers say over and over again when a listing agent misrepresents a property or the view with the wrong photos. This is what buyers often think of as dishonest photos.

You cannot sell a home with dishonest photos to buyers who come expecting something better. I believe the best way to depict your home in the MLS with photos is to do so absolutely honestly. This means show all the good and show all the bad. Buyers are going to find out anyway, right? You cannot fool buyers with photographs.

Poor Photos

Your listing agent could have plenty of photos, and she could have the right photos and the right perspectives, but if she has poor quality photos, you can still lose buyers as they don't get a good feel for your home and property. If they don't think it is right based on poor photos, they may never look at it.

I've already talked about photo equipment with respect to representing a property honestly and completely, but good equipment is needed to capture great photos inside and out.

A good camera, a good lens, good flash lighting, good stationary lighting, and good reflectors may all be needed, depending on the subject property. This is not the place to teach listing agents what kind of equipment to purchase, but I will say that rounding out the equipment list to take the kind of photos buyers expect and hope to find will run the cost of equipment into the thousands, not hundreds.

Listing agents are generally not trained to use this kind of equipment, and they are not inclined to invest the money. While that may sound like an excuse for listing agents, it isn't. Either they should invest in the equipment and learn to use it, or they should hire a professional real estate photographer every time. Most do neither.

Hiring a professional photographer does not necessarily solve all your photo issues. A pro will take good basic photos with good equipment, but he does that for a starter price of maybe $200. He will not do high quality photo editing for that price. That will typically cost several times as much as the basic package, and listing agents are rarely willing to pay for that service up front when they don't even know if they will sell your home.

Buyers depend on good photos when they are looking online. If your home doesn't have great photos, you may miss the most qualified buyers who would pay the highest price for your home.

One last important detail on the subject of getting great photos. Good lighting is one of the keys to getting great photos, and that often means taking multiple photos of the same location with a camera on a tripod, and using multiple flash photography.

A photo that really pops and can make buyers get excited is often one that consists of photo masks and layers to arrive at a true and accurate depiction of a scene. This means lighting dark areas under kitchen counters or in corners or in rooms in the background, and softening the light in other areas, especially windows. This requires extensive photo editing with expensive software. Again this is not something listing agents are trained to do.

Having said all of this, it should be no surprise that more than 50% of all photos in MLS listings are either insufficient in number, the wrong photos, or they are poor photos. It is rare that a listing agent nails all three of these. I actually think that as many as 85% of all MLS listings suffer from one, two, or all three of these shortcomings.

Clearly good photos are important. No one doubts that, but buyers want excellent photos that accurately represent your property. They don't want to be disappointed when they come to see a home. Not only are photos in the MLS important, but good photos are also used to create virtual tours, which are marketed in their own way.

One just cannot overemphasize the importance of good photos. I strongly urge you to make this one of the qualifications you require of a listing agent.

You'll be glad you did.

Videos Are Important

Everything I have written about photos could also be said about videos, and a full discussion of video production, equipment, editing, and optimization and marketing really would require another chapter. Actually, an entire book could easily be written on that topic alone, it's that important. As a home seller, you don't need a course on video production and marketing, at least not here, but your listing agent should also be a videographer, or should hire one.

---

[1] MLS stands for multiple listing service.

[2] Secret No. 18. The number one flaw in MLS listings are poor photos, insufficient photos, or the wrong photos. Make sure your listing agent has this covered with professional quality photos. My estimate is that 85% of MLS listings do not.

[3] It's not hard to do your own analysis of MLS photos. Just do a simple MLS search of any public MLS site of typical 3 bedroom, 2 bath homes, and scroll through 20 or more listings, and see for yourself what percentage of those listings have as many photos as possible of the right areas that buyers want to see, and that are high quality photos that represent the property well. From this examination of these 20 listings, were you able to get an accurate feel for each of the properties or were you left wondering? Increase the accuracy of your statistical study by increasing the number of listings in your sample.

Chapter 11
Accept Only Unambiguous Offers

Your listing agent should draft clear and unambiguous contract language. Your agent should also help you negotiate the best possible price and terms, and assist you through the due diligence process all the way to closing. There will inevitably be some challenging and adversarial issues that come up with the buyer in this process, and the single most important person apart from you in the transaction who can either kill your transaction or save it is your agent. Of course, from the buyer's side, the buyer's agent can also either kill or facilitate.

Using the English language to communicate clearly and without ambiguity is not as common as you would think in the real estate business. This is very fundamental, but it is one of the greatest weaknesses of real estate agents I've seen in three decades in real estate. I have seen language in addendums that would make you laugh, or cry if you were a party to the transaction. Ambiguous or poorly drafted language could cost you your transaction, or it could cost you thousands of dollars.

I got an email from another agent, and I had no idea what she was trying to tell me. You cannot afford sloppy English in your communications or in your real estate agreement. You cannot afford an agent who has not mastered drafting clear language in your contract or who cannot email or talk clearly with others about your transaction. Many lawyers make a good living because people draft poor contracts that leave too much open for dispute.

My daughter and I have a hobby. We watch for reader board signs that have misspelled words or have unintended meanings. Some are hilarious, and if you watch for them, you'll be surprised how many you see now. Signs that are screwed up is one thing, but your real estate documents and all the communications between your agent and all the other parties in your transaction must not be like that reader board that everyone laughs at.

Chapter 12
Handling The Home Inspection

I always recommend that buyers hire home inspectors, and every buyer should pop the $450 to get a thorough home inspection, but there are some important things to know about what home inspectors don't tell you. This is not a matter of honesty or professionalism, because the home inspectors I'm talking about all have incredible credentials and knowledge, and they are all honest and are able to find everything and anything wrong with a home. Even with all this good news, home inspections today are causing tremendous problems for sellers. This chapter explains what that problem is and how to approach a home inspection.

The Problem

The problem is that some home inspectors are scarring buyers with the language used in their reports, and I don't mean just raising concerns. I mean scarring them over minor or typical wear and tear items in a home that do not need immediate repair. But because of the language used in the report, buyers are convinced something terrible is going to happen or that it could happen soon, that someone could be seriously hurt or killed.

So buyers are going back to the negotiating table and demanding that sellers repair items that the sellers would not normally address for maybe 10 years or longer. Essentially buyers are demanding that used homes that are 20 or 30 years old be put in the same condition as a brand new home (with respect to roofs, flooring, appliances, heating systems, decks, and so on). Sellers are getting frustrated and angry at having to spend thousands of dollars for repairs that they feel are not necessary. "After all," sellers say, "I'm selling a used home, not a brand new home."

I'm not talking about the critical repairs that absolutely must be made or that are going to be required for a loan or structural integrity or a serious safety issue. Of course, it is more than appropriate and necessary for a home inspector to address those critical items, and it is appropriate for the buyer and seller to negotiate how to handle such repairs. I'm talking about the unnecessary repairs that create a nightmare scenario for a buyer and a seller, and threatens to kill the entire transaction.

The fault does not lie with buyers who are relying on the professionals they hire to give them good advice. The fault does not lie with sellers who end up having to spend money for unnecessary repairs. The fault lies within the home inspection industry, or perhaps upon individual home inspectors who are applying industry standards, interpretations, and their own phrases without providing buyers with full explanations that will put exaggerated or scary warnings in context. Let's look at the standards in the industry.

The Appraiser's Standard

There are really three inspection standards. The first is the appraisal standard. Here an appraiser for a bank or mortgage company is looking for structural and mechanical problems or other issues with the home that effect its security for the value of the loan. That makes sense, because the appraiser's client is the bank, not the buyer. An appraiser is not looking at appearances. He's not trying to find fault with a property. He's looking at structural and code compliance that effect the value and therefore the security of a loan.

The Home Inspector's Standard

The second standard is the home inspector's standard. Here the home inspector is trying to find anything and everything that might be or could be wrong with the home. Even minutiae that the appraiser would not care about are in the home inspector's report. His report can include notes that something might need further inspection by a specialized expert. A home inspector will make a note that there "may be indicia of" something. In other words, there may be signs that there could be something to look into further. That is a perfectly good idea, but that idea can kill a perfectly good transaction.

One inspector made a note of three tiny ant trails in a crawl space as possible moisture ants that could cause damage to a home, and recommended that the buyer consider having a pest inspector to investigate. But there were no ants present, and there was no indication of any ants in any of the beams or wood in the crawl space. There was no dry rot and no structural issues. The inspector's note in his report caused a great deal of consternation with the buyer who started panicking about the possibility of termites, spiders overtaking the home, snakes lurking in the crawl space, and whether the seller should be required to hire a company to spray the entire property. Meanwhile, there was no sign of any pests whatsoever.

A person might laugh a little at that kind of buyer response, but it happens all the time. Words have meaning, and we all have neurological associations that connect words, feelings, emotions, and fears.

When an inspector recommends that a pest inspection be done, of course a buyer's mind is going to go places it should not go. My point is that there is a huge gap in the use and intended meaning of words between a home inspector and a buyer. Some home inspectors are not helping bridge that gap. If anything, they are making it worse as they are fearful of their own legal liabilities.

After that report followed numerous emails, phone calls, tense feelings, legal forms flying back and forth between the Realtors and their clients, and questions about whether the transaction would make it to closing. All because of a minor note in a report that really did not have to be there. The home inspector considered his note kind of a footnote with little significance, but none of the parties considered his notation insignificant. And therein lies the problem.

Inspectors and appraisers have a job to do, and they do their jobs well, but a home inspector can and often does "scare the hell" out of buyers. They know this, but they feel an obligation to include the language in their reports, thinking they are necessary to protect them from legal liabilities.

The Average Person Standard

The third standard is the one you and I would use as non-experts who think logically. We look at a beam under a deck that has some small rotted section, but that part of the beam does not weaken the structural integrity of the deck, and yet we can jump up and down on the deck. It is as solid as any deck. That is largely because the deck has a lot of other structural support, and the beam is not the only structural support.

Is the rotten section of the beam a "safety issue?" The inspector will call it a safety issue and recommend repair without specifying what kind of repair or how extensive. He would justifiably point out it is not his job to discuss the repair or what the repair should entail. His job is to simply point out the potential issues. If he was a contractor, he may share a rough estimate.

The problem for a seller is that the buyer is hearing "safety issue" and to a buyer that sounds very threatening, and something that needs immediate attention or someone will end up in the hospital or dead. Yet based on the standard that you and I use, we might say the deck is good for many years to come. And sometimes a seller hires a third party contractor who agrees.

Because of the language in the home inspection report, the buyer will feel like the deck needs immediate repair and will typically demand the seller repair it at the seller's cost. But for the rest of us, that would not be necessary, and the deck could be good for many years. Still the home inspector feels legally obligated and is trained to use the words, "safety issue."

This is one example, but the point is home inspectors are unintentionally scaring buyers and creating unnecessary repairs for sellers. The result is often a nightmare scenario thrown into the laps of the buyers and sellers and their Realtors. Everyone is brought back to negotiate all over again on what can be repairs costing thousands of dollars. The seller may have talked to an independent contractor who says the repairs are not necessary, and could be done in the years ahead, but the buyer is thinking, "Oh my God. I can't live in this house." The home inspector never intended such results, but this is what keeps happening over and over again.

All of this is happening because of the different legal and regulatory standards, and because everyone is terrified of getting sued and ending up in an expensive nightmare called a lawsuit. I should also state what I think is obvious—this is not the fault of the home inspectors. They are stuck with what they are taught in their industry and by the legal liabilities they are told are threatening them.

Termites and Pests

Californians are used to doing termite inspections. As one of my California clients said, "Every home in California has termites." Of course, he was exaggerating, but the point is if you say the word, "pests," or "possible pest infestation," in a home inspection in Washington, buyers from California have an emotional switch that gets flipped, and they have all kinds of visions, none of which are pretty. What they don't know is that termites are extremely rare in the some areas, like Sequim and Port Angeles in Washington, and home inspectors regularly use references to pests in the boilerplate of their reports. But Californians don't know that, so they get very nervous when the words are used.

The Building Code

And when a home inspector states that something in the home is not up to the modern building code, he also has just rung another bell for Californians. I understand that every home in California that is sold must be brought up to the modern code, no matter how old. That is not true in Washington. In Washington when a home is built, it must satisfy code requirements at that time, but there is no requirement that homes be constantly upgraded based on changes in the International Building Code. That is a requirement in California, but it is not a requirement in Washington.

The point is when a home inspector references

anything not being up to code in his report, he sets off alarms for the buyer, who is assuming that everything must be brought up to code by law. It is not the home inspector's job to identify items in the home that did meet the building code when the home was built, but today do not meet the new code requirements enacted since the home was built. A home inspector is not a code inspector, but some inspectors have blurred the line, and they are creating havoc in this area between buyers and sellers, especially for buyers from California.

The Tension is Real

Whether I have made my case persuasively or not, I know what I am saying is true, because I see the tension created between buyers and sellers all the time, and for nearly every sale. The solution is not easy, because home inspectors feel like they are caught between a rock and a hard place in terms of liabilities, and they feel obligated to use the phrases that scare people so badly.

For the times that people need to be scared, that's fine, but in a majority of sales today, those phrases are having an unnecessary but serious deleterious affect on buyers and sellers. The fix is really up to the home inspection industry, not me or anyone else, but I hope that by bringing this issue to the forefront, the home inspection industry will begin to address it appropriately.

Part of the answer may already be in place, and that is found in the Washington Administrative Code section which describes in great detail what home inspectors' responsibilities are. It also includes definitions. If all home inspectors were in strict compliance with these WAC provisions, perhaps we would have less tension between buyers and sellers.

My recommendation to clients is to make sure you have wise advisers in your corner. Know when a repair that is identified in a home inspector's report is just there because he is legally bound to use scary language and when it really does need repair because it presents an immediate danger.

You could also make it clear to the buyer during the initial offer and counteroffer phase what your financial limit will be on inspection repairs. That alone could make a big difference in reducing the tension after the inspection is completed.

The real purpose of a home inspection report in Washington should be to discover serious problems with a home that would require a buyer to terminate, not to nickel and dime a seller who already feels like he negotiated his lowest possible price. The best time for a buyer to negotiate the price is in the beginning with the offer and counteroffer.

Chapter 13
The Biggest Problem for Buyers

What is the biggest problem home buyers face in this real estate market? The recurring problem and the number one problem by far is at the lender end of a transaction. I recently had a client who planned to buy a home in Sequim for a long time. When the time came, we looked at his short list of homes and we did find the perfect home. He had a nearly perfect credit score and a 30% down payment. The home inspection went smoothly, the septic inspection passed, the well inspection passed with flying colors, and we proceeded toward closing. Until the problem.

The out-of-town lender didn't order the appraisal until a week before closing. That meant there would not be enough time for the appraiser to physically inspect the property, compile his data, and complete and submit his appraisal report to the bank. Even after he submitted it, the bank's loan underwriter needs time to review it.

We would need a closing extension. Big problem. The sellers had an FHA loan and if we went one day past the end of the month, the sellers would have to make another month's payment, and these FHA loans do not prorate interest. So one day past the end of the month meant another $1,500 mortgage payment. The seller refused to pay it, saying the buyer's lender caused the delay. The buyer refused to pay it saying it was the seller's own loan that required an additional payment.

In another transaction I sold a home to a buyer who qualified and was approved for the loan. The appraisal came in good, right at the purchase price. Then the underwriter decided he didn't like the comps on the appraisal report, so he killed the loan.

And in another transaction, the buyer was eminently qualified for the loan, the appraisal came in above the purchase price, and all inspections were good. But two days before closing, the underwriter complained about something that had never showed up before. It was an old debt, but not even my client's debt. He co-signed a second position home loan for his son years earlier. The son's home was later foreclosed, and it was the second loan that was wiped out by the foreclosure of the first. My client's loan underwriter would not fund the loan until that old debt was resolved, even though it was no longer a legally enforceable debt. This was another lender issue that threatened to kill a transaction at the 11th hour.

Of course buyers must be proactive and diligent to get to closing on any real estate transaction, but there are some things totally outside their control, and some of those things crop up at the 11th hour. Life is full of uncertainties, and so is the real estate business.

Chapter 14
The Closing Date is a
Moving Target

The closing date in your real estate contract is intended as a firm closing date, but as a practical matter closings are extended all the time. Buyers, sellers, mortgage brokers, appraisers, underwriters, title companies, and escrow companies all look at the closing date as a target. Under Washington State case law, and the case law in every state I believe, if a transaction cannot close on the exact closing date through no fault of the buyer, the closing may be extended a reasonable period of time, and the seller is still under contract and obligated to close. Recently many transactions missed the original closing date and the closing must be extended one, two, or three times. Why?

I had a transaction in which the closing date had to be extended four times. Not one of the extensions was the fault of the buyer or the seller, nor were any of the extensions the fault of the mortgage broker, nor the title or escrow companies. So who was at fault? Why did this transaction need four extensions to close?

One of the reasons this closing was extended was that the appraiser took a long time to get to the property and do his appraisal. Then he took a couple more weeks to get his written report submitted to the lender. Two days before the closing date, the underwriter for the lender said the appraisal report indicated the water was not turned on in the house. That didn't make any sense to the rest of us, because no one shut the water off.

The underwriter said he would not fund the loan without the water on, which was ridiculous. After a volley of phone calls between nearly everyone involved in the transaction, and many emails back and forth for two days, we learned the water actually was on. It was the appraiser who made a mistake in his written report. He had checked the wrong box.

Another extension was needed because of items noted in the home inspection report that needed to be repaired, and that meant entering a whole new phase of negotiations (and paperwork) with the seller. Any repairs require independent bids, repair work, and proof of the repairs, and then the appropriate paperwork must be approved and signed by the buyer and seller, and the underwriter must approve the repairs.

All of that can add weeks to a closing date.

And another extension was needed when the lender could not fund the loan on the exact closing date, so we extended by two days, but the lender did not get their package to the escrow company in time for overnight deliveries of the closing documents, so we had to extend again.

Closing Extensions and Moving Trucks

When the closing date is a moving target, trying to plan your own move can be frustrating. Here's where it can get quite challenging. If you are selling, you will plan so your moving trucks will arrive just prior to the closing date, so you can be out of your home in time for the buyer to move in. Scheduling moving trucks is no small task, and you pay for every day the trucks sit.

If the buyer is coming from another state, they have the same challenge. They schedule their moving trucks to arrive the day of closing, and if closing gets extended, they will be stuck paying for trucks sitting in the driveway. This can be a scheduling nightmare at both ends. Buyers do not want to put things in storage and end up moving twice.

I recommend that buyers work with a very experienced and professional mortgage broker who is local, and both buyer and seller should work with experienced real estate agents who know how to be proactive and who know how to work through complex issues that can and regularly do come up. The truth is, real estate transactions are more difficult today than they have been in the past three decades.

Chapter 15
The 353 Day Short Sale

You probably have heard that a short sale can take a long time to get approved and closed. Try 353 days from the date on the contract to the closing date. Let's call it one year. Since I represented the buyers on this short sale, I know the history of this transaction. Too well.

A short sale is the sale of a home that is upside down. In other words, the home sells for less than the balance of the mortgage, and that requires that the bank agree to take a loss by getting paid less than what they are owed. As a buyer, you might ask why a short sale would take any longer than a regular sale?

I represented buyers from Washington D.C. who had decided to make Sequim their retirement destination. I communicated with them for a period of months before they arrived, and when they arrived, we looked at about eight homes, but they didn't get excited about any of them. Then while driving past a home I had shown before but was not on our list, I casually mentioned that this home was vacant and if they would like to see it, we could. To my surprise they fell in love with this home immediately.

The prior owner had paid $1.2 million for this gorgeous home which had quite a water view, and now it was on the market for under $600,000 as a short sale. My clients headed back to Washington D.C. and after giving this home some more thought, they decided to make an offer, which we did. Unfortunately, another buyer had stepped into the picture and made an offer that was accepted.

My clients were thinking they lost their dream home, but we decided to submit a backup offer. After a few months, the buyers in first position decided to walk away based on their dissatisfaction with some minor issues in the home inspection report, so my clients were suddenly in first position, and we started the short sale application process.

In a short sale it is the seller who must satisfy their bank, and essentially that means their bank must have proof that the seller cannot make the mortgage payments anymore, and that the seller is essentially financially destitute. If the seller has any financial resources to pay the mortgage off, the bank will not agree to a short sale. The seller must submit a thorough short sale package with financial statements, bank statements, and a narrative explanation called a "Financial Hardship Letter."

In this transaction all of these communications were between the listing agent, her seller, and the bank. As a buyer's agent, I had no authority to be involved in that process. We assumed the listing agent was handling the paperwork properly and facilitating the process as quickly as practical. For reasons that were not explained, the short sale process started and ended on three different occasions over a period of about nine months.

What my buyers and I did not know was that the listing agent did not know how to prosecute a short sale, and she made multiple mistakes that delayed the bank's approval several times. She did not use their short sale software correctly, and she missed some bank deadlines in completing paperwork. She also did not have a direct line of communication with her own client.

During the process the bank ordered an appraisal, and we were all elated to find out that the appraisal came in close to the price that the buyer and seller had agreed upon. If the appraisal had come in much higher, the bank would not have agreed to the contract price.

Weeks turned into months. It was a very frustrating experience for my clients and me. After 300 days had passed we felt like we were in a twilight zone. We couldn't get straight answers from the listing agent, and we could not get any answers from the bank since we were never allowed to communicate directly with the bank or the company they hired to handle the short sale. We didn't even have names or phone numbers for the correct contacts. But the listing agent didn't seem to either.

Finally after 353 days, we closed.

A short sale should not be handled by an agent who doesn't have short sale experience. It is definitely not an arena in which an agent should expect to learn by trial and error. That's how you can get a 353 day short sale.

While I have the experience to handle a short sale from the listing or selling end of a transaction, do not attempt to handle a short sale myself. I always bring in a full time professional short sale negotiator, one of the best in the country, and that's how I get short sales completed in a matter of months instead of a year. A short sale should not take more than three months.

Chapter 16
MLS Marketing &
The Twilight Zone

There's a lot of confusion about how the MLS (multiple listing service) works, and how listings are put on the Internet. The purpose of this chapter is to help you understand exactly how your listing is put on the Internet through the local MLS, how listing syndication works, and how all of this fits into marketing your property.

When a home is listed, the listing agent inputs that listing information and the photos into the local MLS. As soon as it is saved as a[1] completed and active listing, all other local agents who are dues-paying members on the subscription side of the MLS will be able to find it and show it.

The next day the listing will show up on all the public MLS sites with an IDX data feed from the same MLS. An IDX data feed is technical language, but in plain language it includes the data and photos from the listing that are uploaded and viewable on public MLS sites.

A public MLS site is the consumer site that buyers use to search for homes and land. These are the sites that agents (or their brokerage) own or lease, and these are the sites that show all the local listings. Of course, agents hope their MLS sites will generate buyer leads for them.

With that goal, most agents have been instructed by the so-called "experts" to force buyers to register after three or five searches in order to capture those leads. What the "experts" don't realize is that consumers don't like being forced to register and give all their confidential information to a website and an agent they do not know.

Any site that promotes your listing should freely offer that information to any and all potential buyers without requiring them to register. Chasing buyers away is not a good marketing strategy if the goal is to give your listing information to as many people as possible.

Not All Public MLS Sites Are User Friendly

A public MLS site doesn't have all the information that the agent-only subscription side has, but it has most of the information buyers need. Not all public MLS sites are the same, and not all provide all the information buyers want, including data like "days on market" (DOM), and current "Status" (active, pending, short sale contingent on bank approval, etc.). Not all public MLS sites give buyers the ability to search more than one MLS service from a single location. In addition, navigation, mapping features, and the ability to get e-alerts are not all the same. Accuracy and convenience are substantially different on public MLS sites.[2]

There's another important aspect to a great public MLS site. Consumers like sites that are easy to navigate. In other words, when it comes to searching for properties, saving favorites, using advance search tools, and so on, the navigation on an MLS site should be intuitive. Consumers who use the Internet are developing habits and expectations of where something will be on a site, so their eyes look to a certain location, and their fingers seek to click on the mouse at the right time.

Then there is the psychology of colors. There are colors that sell, and there are colors that push people away emotionally. All of this needs to be part of the original design and programming of an MLS site. Unfortunately, programmers at large corporations are not typically able to get inside the heads of agents' buyers, so there is a fairly significant gap in what programmers build and what buyers want. That's true when agents are stuck with a corporate MLS site, or when agents don't have the technological expertise on board to build the right kind of MLS site for clients in their market niche.

Your listing agent should have one of the best public MLS sites, and it should access 100% of all the listings so buyers can find every home, and it should be 100% accurate using the source data from the local agent's MLS listing sheets. It should be easy to navigate but very powerful as a search tool for buyers. This only describes a small percentage of the public MLS sites out there. It may sound logical, but few are designing and programming their MLS sites to do all this. It makes a big difference to buyers, and it's buyers we want to reach to sell your home.[3]

Once your listing is entered in the MLS, it will become visible on all other local agents' public MLS sites,[4] which means it will reach every buyer searching every one of these sites. That usually means that your listing shows up on a couple hundred public MLS sites, and that is a good thing.

Your listing will also be syndicated from the MLS to hundreds of other publicly accessed real estate sites. Zillow, Trulia, Realtor.com, Homes.com, and many other sites will either access the IDX data feed directly from the MLS, or they will use automatic scrapping software to pull the data and photos off various Internet sites and compile it so they can use it on their own sites. There are no human beings involved in this process. It is all automated and usually done during the night when there is less Internet traffic.

Syndications Are Not Always Good

Many of the national sites that syndicate listings like this are doing so illegally without the permission of the local MLSs. Why don't local MLSs sue services that steal the MLS data? Local MLSs and the real estate associations do not have the funds to hire attorneys and fight billion dollar companies who could drive them into the ground in legal fees.

Some agents would argue that they don't want to stop the illegal syndications, that they want their clients' listings to be broadcast in as many places as possible. That's a good argument, but there are a couple of pretty big negatives to the syndication process.

The first is that services like Zillow that promote your listing without your permission and without your listing agent's permission often get the information terribly wrong. Agents around the country have a regular conversation going on about how defective so much of the data is in Zillow.

What kind of information does Zillow get

wrong? Their Zestimates are often terribly wrong. I had a home listed and which sold for $770,000, and Zillow stated its value was $440,000. That's off by almost 50%. Zillow's automatic software regularly gets the listing price wrong, shows homes for sale when they are not for sale, and lists homes for sale that were sold two years earlier.

How can Zillow and other syndication sites get your property information so screwed up? Remember they are using automated scrapping programs that pull information about your property from various public sites. All those sites with information about your property, like the county tax assessor's website, have fields designed and programmed for their specific purpose. Those data field names do not necessarily match up with the data field names on Zillow's real estate pages. So the software tries to match numbers up with data fields that have different names.

Sometimes that works if the various names have been programmed into Zillow's software, but other times it does not. The software is running 24/7 regardless, and this is how you can end up with a full page of information about your property with mistakes or grossly incorrect information.

All that incorrect information makes for a good argument that illegal syndications should be stopped. But there's another reason that sites like Zillow do a lot of harm. You and your listing agent lose control of the information that is publicly broadcast to the world about your property.

Buyers regularly get the wrong impression about properties, and that's part of losing control of marketing your own property effectively. Many buyers look at homes on Zillow and see Zestimates that are 20% to 50% below the listed price, and they automatically assume that your home is grossly over priced, and they move on, thanks to Zillow. They never come to look at your home because of that. This is probably the best argument that syndications should not be allowed without your permission.

Listing Syndications Are Out of Control

Unfortunately, the entire process is so out of control, no one can stop it. There may be hundreds of sites syndicating your listing without your permission, and with absolutely no accountability to you or your listing agent for the accuracy (or inaccuracy) of the information about your home. That ought to bother any homeowner trying to sell their home. From a practical perspective, there's nothing we can do about these syndications. It's happening all over the country, and it's out of control.

Many buyers are using Zillow because they like some of the features and the interface. If they understood how bad much of the data is, they might be inclined to use a local MLS site that is 100% accurate, but buyers searching for their next home don't know all these things. So they continue to use Zillow and get the wrong impression about a lot of properties for sale. It is a terrible disservice to home sellers like you.

If Buyers Only Knew The Truth

Buyers often think Zillow is a public MLS service for buyers, but it is not an approved MLS site. Local real estate associations and MLSs around the country have not all given Zillow permission to use their data. County tax offices, which is where the source real estate tax records reside, have not consented to Zillow using their data. Zillow uses all this data without permission and without paying the owners for the use of this data. So who are Zillow's customers, and who pays Zillow?

The way Zillow makes money is by selling space and leads to real estate agents. Agents are Zillow's number one customers, because agents are the ones who write those monthly checks.

And agents can't write those checks fast enough. Zillow is using high pressure sales tactics, and what I believe are misrepresentations to sell its service to agents. For example, Zillow promoted the heck out of one agent's claim to have sold $100 million in real estate from Zillow leads. Of course, that is ridiculous. That is impossible for one agent to do. It's not even remotely possible. He may have sold $100 million in gross volume with hundreds of agents working in his brokerage or brokerages, but even then you can bet all those sales were not generated exclusively from Zillow leads. That's about as likely as me winning the Powerball lottery. His claim was clearly that he alone sold $100 million from Zillow leads.

This was promoted by Zillow, and Zillow paid affiliates around the country who promoted this same exaggeration with videos, articles, and webinars. What do you think real estate agents around the country said? Like sheep to the slaughter, they clamored to buy the exclusive rights to a zip code in their market. Zillow figured out how to create an artificial shortage by limiting how many times they would sell each zip code. They put high prices on each zip code, and sat back while agents competed to get in line to buy zip codes.

And these zip codes are not cheap. They cost hundreds to thousands per month for each zip code, depending on the market. Zillow's campaign to sell agents zip codes has been so incredibly successful that there are virtually no zip codes available in most markets around the country. Not only have all zip codes sold out in all good markets, there are long waiting lists to buy zip codes. The only way an agent can buy one is if another agent lets his subscription expire. Some of these zip code waiting lists are so long, Zillow is guaranteed to have these zip codes sold out for many years to come.

Perhaps now you are getting a clearer picture of Zillow's business model and why neither you as a seller, nor the buyers are really any concern at all to Zillow. You are not directly part of their business income, but they are using your property information without your permission to generate billions of dollars for Zillow. They are making so much money, they are buying their largest competitor, Trulia.

I've shared this with a more detailed explanation than you might find anywhere else, but I think it's important for home sellers to know how the listing and syndication process works. But this explanation can also help alleviate some frustration when you see your listing on Zillow or other syndication sites with all kinds of bad information. Don't blame your listing agent. He didn't do it. Zillow did without his permission.

The Zillow Free-For-All

Zillow is generating lots of leads for agents, especially in metropolitan markets. Agents are paying big buck for these leads, but agents feel like Zillow is a ruthless mistress. The reason is that Zillow makes agents pay thousands of dollars every month to purchase leads for a zip code, but then Zillow distributes those leads to multiple agents at the same time.

What this means is that buyers get inundated with phone calls and emails from agents who are desperately trying to capture those leads they have dearly paid for. Zillow is selling the same leads to many agents at the same time. So here is exactly what Zillow tells agents to do: Be the first agent to call, and you'd better call within a few minutes of the Zillow inquiry. Do you see what a free-for-all this has become? What a racket Zillow has going.

Sellers are on the outside of all this, so they don't know about the chaos Zillow is creating for all of us. But now you know. Unfortunately, there's nothing any of us can do about Zillow. They are the elephant in the room, at least until something better comes along.

Two MLS Services?

In some areas of the U.S. there is more than one MLS service. When there are two MLSs in one market, that can create a problem marketing a property. To explain how this works and what you need to know, I'll use a real example from my own real estate market.

Many home sellers in Sequim and Port Angeles, Washington do not know there are two completely separate MLS services. The original MLS service in Clallam County is the Olympic Listing Service (OLS). This is a company owned by a large financial services conglomerate based in Florida. Almost all local agents are members of the OLS, which means that nearly 100% of the local listings are in the OLS. The OLS is only in a small number of counties in the state.

The second MLS is the Northwest MLS. This is the largest MLS in the state of Washington, and it covers the largest counties in the state, including Pierce County and King County (the entire Seattle-Tacoma Metropolis). Most of the agents in the state are members of the NWMLS, and that means over 25,000 agents. Only 55% of the local Clallam County agents are members of the NWMLS. In other words, while all local agents are members of the OLS, only half are members of the NWMLS.

Seattle area agents who are not members of the OLS cannot access the agent-only information in the OLS MLS, which includes information about showing the property, who to call, whether the property is vacant or occupied, and whether an appointment is necessary. Seattle agents cannot become members of the OLS without paying a membership fee to the local real estate association, which they are not willing to do when they occasionally want to show a local property. Agents from outside the area feel that local agents are not very cooperative when it comes to allowing them to access the showing instructions and agent-only information.

What happens when you have two MLSs? You have to post your listing in both of them to get exposure to the largest number of agents and the largest number of buyers those agent may have for a home like yours. Local agents access local listings through their subscription site to the OLS, but the thousands of agents outside Clallam County who are members of the NWMLS, not the OLS, do not have access to your showing information. They could look at one of the local agent's public MLS sites to see your listing, but they are only seeing what the rest of the public sees. Most public MLS sites don't show DOM (days on market), and most don't show if the listing is pending or contingent (instead showing all of them as "active" to generate more potential leads).

What makes matters more complicated is that some agents from Seattle and other areas outside Clallam County are listing local properties, but since they are not members of the OLS, those listings are invisible to local agents, and invisible to buyers who are using a local agents public MLS site. They list them only on the NWMLS where they are members.

So if you want to find all properties listed for sale in Clallam County, you have to access a public MLS site with the OLS listings and another one with the NWMLS listings. Then you will be looking at 100% of the listed properties for sale. I programmed a public MLS that does just that--allows buyers to search one site by address or MLS number, and no matter which listing agent has it listed and no matter if that agent is only a member of the OLS or only a member of the NWMLS, this site will show the listing.[5]

Of course, the best scenario for marketing your listing would be one powerful clean MLS where all agents input their listings and where all the public MLS sites will show 100% of the local listings. For the time being agents in Clallam County are unable to agree on only one MLS, so we will continue to have a bifurcated MLS system. In my opinion that is not in the best interest of consumers, either buyers or sellers.

I recommend listing your properties with an agent who is a member of both systems.[6] You need the most exposure to the most agents and the most buyers, and right now the only way to do that is to get it posted in both MLSs.

---

[1] A county tax assessor's database of properties is collected and owned by

the county. In order to access that data and re-publish it, one would leg
be required to sign a written agreement with the county government.
Foreclosure.com, RealtyTrac.com, Zillow.com, among other syndication
sites, have not signed agreements with Clallam County, where I live. That
means they illegally collect the information off the Internet. That also
means they don't have access to the accurate database fields or names.
Hence, a lot of accuracy is lost in the translation.

[2] Secret No. 19. One of your listing agent's most important marketing tools
is his public MLS site. Have you examined it, and do you know what to
look for? Be sure about this, because it is very important.

[3] My MLS sites are designed and programmed to do all these things,
because I am intensely focused on connecting with qualified buyers. Only
when I give buyers the best customer service experience on my MLS site
am I also giving you the best marketing service as a home seller.

[4] It usually takes overnight before a new listing (or a change in a listing)
shows up on a public MLS site. The subscription side of an MLS site is
available immediately to all member agents, but public MLS sites normally
update at night when there is less Internet traffic. This means the public
won't see a new listing or a change until the day after.

[5] I created an MLS site that agents on the Seattle side of the Strait (and
anyone outside Clallam County) can use to access all OLS and NWMLS
listings with one search. Seattle agents know that this brokerage is absolutely delighted to work with them, and if they can sell any of our listings, we
are not only a cooperative brokerage, we will help them coordinate their
buyer's inspections and due diligence so they don't have to drive so far. This
is an example of putting the client at the center of the Universe.

[6] Secret No. 20. If you are listing in a market where there is more than one
MLS, make sure your listing agent is going to put your property in both
MLSs. Why would you not want the greatest possible exposure to other
agents and all their clients?

Chapter 17
What is Good Customer Service in Real Estate?

What is good customer service in the real estate business? How would you define good customer service? I have some ideas on that subject, and I'll share them here for your consideration.

Customer service does not exist in a vacuum. It is a function of many factors that make up a business and the people. What are those factors?

Good customer service is built on a business model that puts clients first. This is huge. Some businesses are not focused on their customers. They have their own agendas. How they market, how they sell, and how they treat their customers is based on the almighty dollar. Granted, making money is what a business is supposed to do, but when money making becomes the dominant philosophy that rules all other decisions, you don't have a system built on good customer service.

That kind of business model compromises customer service in a hundred little ways. Customers are generally happy as long as their transactions go smoothly without a hitch, but if there are difficult issues to work through, they often find out their agent is missing in action.

However, a business model that is designed with the customer at the center of everything has a dramatically different approach to customer service. Every question is answered with the customer's best interest in mind. Agents have the knowledge and experience to handle anything that comes up. They also have the courtesy and professionalism to give their clients the best customer service. In this model, not only is customer service consistently great, customers are often giddy about the customer service their agents give them.

<u>Good customer service requires people who genuinely care about their clients</u>. That care must be more than just talk. An agent who puts their clients at the center of the Universe will do everything with their clients' best interests in mind, even walking away from a commission if necessary. And the service is not limited by a strict set of rules. You would never hear an agent say, "No, that's not in my job description." These agents often talk about how they love their

clients. There's nothing they wouldn't do for their clients.[1]

<u>Good customer service is responsive to clients, pays attention to their needs, and helps them through every issue they need resolved</u>. When a client makes a telephone call to their agent, their agent either answers the call or calls back fairly quickly. When a client emails their agent, they get a responsive email quickly.

There's an important exception to a quick response as a standard of good service. An agent might be busy when you call or email, and he simply cannot respond immediately. If he is out showing houses and does not see your message until late that evening, he might not have an opportunity to intelligently answer your question until the next morning.

And there is a challenge for the top producing agent in handling large volumes of inquiries. If he gets behind by 24 hours or even 12 hours, he may have hundreds of messages to filter through. Your message could get missed, not because your agent doesn't work hard, and not because he doesn't care about you, but because of the shear volume that snowballs if he gets behind.

If your agent has a successful marketing system, and as a result he is very busy responding to buyer inquiries, don't be angry with him if he is not as quick responding to you. You should be glad his business model is generating a lot of buyer activity. At the same time, he should not be ignoring you. Good customer service manages all clients intelligently and reasonably.

If you email, and you don't get a response the same day or the next day, don't assume that your agent is unresponsive or ignoring you. Your email may have gone into his spam folder, and he may not have seen it. Even if it did not, many of us now have email management sub-folders, and for a busy agent who gets 200 or more emails every day, an email can get lost in the system.

A good agent can answer questions thoroughly, because he is a real estate expert. Why would anyone hire a real estate agent who is not a real estate expert? If he doesn't immediately know the answer to a unique or esoteric question (or wants to confirm his answer), he finds out and gets back to his client right away.

Not only does good customer service mean all a client's questions get promptly and thoroughly answered, the client feels like the answers were complete and detailed, and their agent has left no stone unturned. They keep getting the feeling that their agent is really watching out for them, and they are very grateful, because they don't normally get this quality of customer service anywhere else.

By the time their transaction closes, they are not only happy with their agent, they are as pleased as they could possibly be. Anything less is just ordinary customer service.

<u>Good customer service is a function of values</u>. There are key values you would expect to be foundational for good customer service. Those values include honesty, integrity, hard work, perseverance, competence, professionalism, loyalty, and a passion to constantly improve one's knowledge and abilities for the sake of his clients. Unfortunately, these values are not as common as one would like to think.

<u>Good customer service depends on the company culture</u>. A real estate brokerage has a culture just like any company does. That culture is created by the owner, and it filters throughout the company and influences everyone who works there. So the question becomes, what is the brokerage culture?

Is the owner kind, generous, devoted to the best interests of all their clients, and passionate about serving others more than putting money in her own pocket in ways that could compromise the clients? Does she bend over backwards to handle every detail for her clients? Will she work overtime to get her clients' work done? Is her commitment to honesty uncompromised? Does she treat everyone equally in the best way possible? Does she constantly seek to improve her real estate knowledge so she can give her clients the highest level of expertise? And does this broker/owner hold all her agents accountable to the highest standards?

All of this together creates a culture of customer service that speaks to the clients in a hundred ways, especially when it is most important. Whatever the culture created by the leadership, it becomes the culture of the brokerage. The thinking and behavior of the leader tends to permeate the entire brokerage, and the longer the same leader runs the company, the more entrenched that culture becomes.

It's amazing, but brokerages tend to assemble agents with similar values and work habits that fit within the culture of the company. That's either good news or bad news for consumers, depending on the culture of the brokerage.

Do not take good customer service for granted, because it is not so common.

---

[1] There's a lot an agent can do to help her clients, and good customer service goes above and beyond what the average agent does, but this doesn't mean an agent will go outside her area of real estate expertise to play the role some other professional should play. For example, if there are legal issues that should be addressed by an attorney, an agent must recom-

mend the client see an attorney.

Chapter 18
How to Have a Great Relationship
With Your Agent

or

How to Avoid a Nightmare

This chapter may be one of the most important chapters in this book. I say that because so many people do not know how to have a good positive relationship with their listing agent. They may know how to have a good relationship with their Dentist, their CPA, and their pizza guy, but when it comes to working with an agent, many people don't know what to expect from a good agent, and many do not know how to relate to their agent in appropriate ways.

In the early '60s when I was still watching cartoons, there was a show called *The Rocky and Bullwinkle Show*. I don't remember much about the show, but I do remember the show always had two titles. There was a positive title, and there was a negative title. The way they presented the two titles, it was like you had a choice which title you wanted to choose. You could choose the positive title or the negative title, but the story line was the same. So in celebration of *The Bull-winkle Show* I gave this chapter two titles. Both titles make a point and tell a story. The flip side of having a wonderful positive relationship with your listing agent is experiencing a nightmare. If we talk about one, we must talk about the other. And like *The Bulwinkle* titles, you get to choose which relationship you want.

The First Key: Hire Right

The first and most important key to having a great relationship with a listing agent, or avoiding a stressful relationship, is to hire the right one. That's what this book is all about, so you should have a good handle on that by the time you get to this chapter. If you ignore everything in this book, if you throw away my 37 years of real estate experience, and you certainly can do that, if you don't use my 26-Point Interview Checklist, and if your discernment meter doesn't work, it will just be a toss of the dice as to whether you get a great agent, a good agent, a mediocre agent, or a bad agent.

When it comes to selling your home, it's not a good time to start gambling. Don't guess. Do not toss the dice. Have a solid strategic plan, and that plan should start with hiring the right agent. Screw this up, and even if you get all the following steps right, you will still have a nightmare looming.

The Second Key: Appropriate Expectations

The second key is to have appropriate expectations about your agent. What is he going to do and what is he not going to do, and how will he communicate with you? This is where a percentage of clients tend to struggle. Some high maintenance clients expect that their agent will constantly inform them of all the ways he markets their property, where and how he does that, how many people have viewed their listing on dozens of different sites and video tours, how many agents have shown their property, and what the feedback is from every single prospective buyer.

Home sellers often get frustrated after months of lack of communications from their listing agent. The problem is they had high expectations that were not met. On one side the home seller is assuming and expecting that their listing agent will regularly and periodically call them and let them know what's going on, email them, and once in a while have a face-to-face. But most listing agents whose entire business model is just listing properties do not include those kinds of time consuming communications in their business plan. The home seller expects much more in communications, but the listing agent has no intention of doing all that communicating. All of that is never discussed. Hence the home seller's disillusionment later.

Perhaps their listing agent didn't know how to include this kind of conversation in the listing appointment, or maybe it just isn't part of that agent's business plan. Maybe the listing agent knows she won't be doing much communicating or even showing the property much, but if she told her client that, she would never get the listing.

As a busy agent, I've struggled with regular and valuable communications to my own listing clients. After many years of doing a pretty good job with most clients but not so great in communicating with others, I finally developed my own checklist with calendar reminders so that I do regularly communicate with my clients in a number of ways. But this takes a system, it takes time, and it takes a lot of self-discipline on my part as a listing agent. I know what I'm doing, and I know I'm very busy marketing seven days a week on behalf of my clients, but they don't know what I'm doing or what is happening in the market as it relates to their property unless I personally talk with them. So this is one of the keys to a successful relationship between an agent and the home seller.

It is important in my opinion for an agent and client to have a good understanding of all these issues when listing a property, so later there won't be misunderstandings and disillusionment. But part of effectively communicating is helping clients understand how things work from the agent's perspective. That's a big reason I wrote this chapter—to help round out a home seller's understanding of what an agent deals with so they can have a positive relationship without lots of bumps along the way.

High Maintenance Clients

There really is such a thing as high maintenance clients. Such clients can be stressful for agents, and certainly time consuming. But high maintenance is not always a bad thing. Many high maintenance clients are just inexperienced and lack knowledge, so they need more questions answered than most, and there may be more hand holding. All that is perfectly fine.

Other high maintenance clients often have questions that never seem to end, like why does Zillow have some information incorrect on their property, why does Trulia show their property the way it does, why can't they find their listing on Craigslist on a particular day, why are some homes selling and this one has not, why is their home not getting more showings, how do syndicated listings work, why isn't my property listed in "such-and-such" magazine, and on and on and on.

I don't mind questions, and agents learn to be

patient and respond to their clients' inquiries. Some questions are certainly good and appropriate, but a good listing agent is quite busy just doing his job to market your property, managing the listings and syndications, the video tours, and communicating with all the people who contact him for information on various properties, marketing on the Internet, writing articles, and so on.

Most high maintenance clients would say they would never expect their agent to teach them everything he knows, but by asking never-ending questions during the term of the listing and constantly challenging their agent, they are doing just that. That's because their agent has to keep explaining why he is doing something or not doing it, how marketing works for this property, and he has to respond to dozens, if not hundreds of other questions.

When a client keeps asking their agent questions and challenging his marketing strategies during the term of the listing, that usually stems from a lack of trust. If you've hired the right agent, you are going to have to trust his knowledge, experience, professionalism, and integrity, and that means trusting him to do what needs to be done, and not to do what does not need to be done. He doesn't need you constantly questioning his competence or his professionalism, assuming he really is competent and professional. You would not have hired him unless you first proved to yourself that he is. Right?

It has been said that trust is something that you earn, and it takes time to earn trust. I believe that is true, but this is why doing your due diligence in the beginning is so darn important. You hire someone who checks out based on my 26-Point Interview Checklist, and you start the relationship with your trust, not mistrust. While trust is earned, you begin by trusting the right person, and you continue to trust unless your agent shows you he is not trustworthy. Your trust is not blind trust in the beginning, because you have done extensive research on your agent before you hired him, and you had plenty of evidence to indicate that he is trustworthy. This is a serious matter, and if your agent is not trustworthy, you need to fire him and find one who is.

The Third Key: Let Your Agent Be Himself

The third key is going to be hard for most home sellers: Let your agent be himself and communicate with you consistent with his own gifts and time and preferences. In other words, don't try to force your agent to become you, or to communicate in exactly the same way you do.

Educators talk about three learning styles: auditory, visual, and kinesthetic. We each tend to learn best within one of these learning preferences. Some people would rather talk on the phone or in person than email something. This is auditory. Some learn best by seeing for themselves. This is visual. And others are touchy and feely and operate out of a higher level of emotions than most people. This is kinesthetic.

You will undoubtedly favor one or two of these learning and communication styles. Your listing agent may operate out of a different style, but it is not entirely fair to try to force your agent to be like you with the same learning and communication style.

If your listing agent knows what he is doing, and why would you hire someone who doesn't, then let him do his job, and that means that he will communicate with you when he has something important and relevant. If you favor an auditory style, and your agent favors a visual style, don't make him call you just to say, "Well, I just want to touch base with you, although I don't have anything to say. Just wanted you to know I'm here." Duh! How silly is that kind of phone call, especially to your agent?

Having said all of that, I would emphasize that I think it is very important for an agent and home seller to sit down in the beginning of the listing term and discuss how they plan to communicate, how often, and what kind of information will be shared. While communication styles may vary, the agent has a duty to communicate regularly with a home seller during the term of the listing. That's why I developed my own checklist and calendaring system to remind me when to update each of my clients. A regular conversation goes a long way to building and maintaining a great relationship.

The Fourth Key: Respect

Always treat your agent with respect. While treating other people with respect comes natural to most of us, I have learned from the real estate school of hard knocks that some people can be inconsiderate and talk down to their agents. That's not a good strategy for building positive relationships.

Here's what I've learned. When a person does not respect another person from the beginning of a relationship, that is the beginning of a relationship that will continue the same pattern until the end. There are some people I choose not to work with because they are going to fill our relationship with stress and anxiety. Why go there? Life is too short for those kinds of relationships.

Great Positive Relationships

If you want a great positive relationship with your agent, you can have that (remember to hire the right agent), but your relationship will only be as good as your own attitude. Are you generous and appreciative of people who work for you? Do you treat them with respect as an equal? Do you withhold judgment when something happens until you can find out the truth, or do you immediately seek a scapegoat with cross hairs on your agent's back? Are you forgiving and kind? Working with a true professional real estate agent who is honest and competent and works hard for you can be a good and positive experience, but half of the responsibility for that depends on your own attitude.

Having said all of this, your agent owes you a number of things, including fiduciary duties, contractual obligations, good ethics, honesty, integrity, competence, and professionalism. And your agent also has a responsibility to treat you with respect, communicate with you regularly as he promised to do, and to maintain a positive relationship with you.

It will take planning and good communications from the beginning, and it also will require that both you and your agent handle all the little issues that normally come up along the way with maturity and patience. Nothing is easy, and selling a home is not easy. The entire process can be challenging, but by working as a team with your agent and maintaining a positive relationship based on trust and honesty, you really can have a great relationship with your agent.

Appendix

What Others Say About Chuck

From California to Sequim. Thanks to Chuck we now own our perfect Sequim retirement home! From the first search on his website, to his informative blog, to his great advice on how and when to make an offer, things could not have gone better. There is no doubt in our minds that should anyone ask us for a recommendation on a Realtor, Chuck's name would be the only one on the list. Thanks, Chuck. Don B.

Bought and Sold. My husband and I were introduced to Chuck online through his blog many years ago. We had been looking at Sequim property on and off through the years with other Realtors before we found Chuck. Chuck's website provides so much information – you really can do your homework and narrow things down. In 2009, we were determined to buy our retirement home in Sequim. We met with Chuck for several house-hunting expeditions. The market was tricky. Not a lot of houses available in a market that was still reeling from the housing bubble.

We could not find what we were looking for, so we decided to build. Chuck patiently guided us through this process. Finally, we found the lot we were looking for in the area we desired. We forged ahead and bought the lot. Chuck's experience living in Sequim for many years and his background as a real-estate lawyer was invaluable in helping us work through this process. Through Chuck we met our builder whose integrity and patience made building our house a pleasure. Turn the clock forward to 2014 and, as we all know, life does not stand still. After building our dream home and loving our home and where we lived, we were hit with a sudden change in life's plan. Having to make a very difficult decision, we decided to sell our retirement home and move on. Without a doubt, Chuck was the Realtor we called to sell our home. This was not an easy decision after all we had gone through to finally get settled in Sequim. Chuck supported us all the way. He was our listing agent. His views on how to list and market a home were right on point. Chuck works round the clock and gets what needs to get done when it needs to get done. He is amazing. Right from the start of the listing, we had a lot of interested buyer activity. We recently closed on the selling of our home - five months after listing. This was our third offer. The first buyer simply backed out. The second buyer had a contingency on the sale of their home but was savvy enough to add a bump clause to get the contract accepted. They got bumped and the third buyer is now the proud and happy owner of our home. None of this could have been done without Chuck's knowledge, integrity, experience and thoughtfulness. Rick & Marilyn

<u>Selling an Estate</u>. I've had the pleasure of working with Chuck over the past three years in selling my parent's estate. It was a tough time to sell during the housing recession, but Chuck always kept things on the positive side. With his real estate law background, he offers sound, practical advice. He helps you along with the process using discussions and reason, rather than opinions and speculations. If Chuck doesn't know the answers, he will get them for you. In several instances, Chuck took the initiative to meet with county officials to get up-to-date facts about zoning and regulations. I was always impressed with his company's tech savvy communications and internet presence: weekly email updates, blogs, videos, links, Linked-in networking, etc. He is truly pioneering the future of buying & selling real estate. Brian M.

<u>Knew How to Sell Property</u>. In our Sequim real estate broker Chuck Marunde we found a Realtor who knew not only how to list a property, but most importantly, he knew how to sell a property. Chuck is very skilled in current technology and uses that skill to advertise your property nationally. We were very

pleased with Chuck, his honesty and integrity. Jerry and Teva

Listed and Bought. I've known Chuck Marunde for several years. My wife and I bought and sold one house through his services, and now have another listed through him for sale. Whether Chuck was representing us as the buyer or seller, I am confident he always had our best interests at heart. He helped us set or negotiate a reasonable price, and made sure there was a clear and open line of communication. He responded rapidly to email and phone calls and always knew the best person to contact for the various services involved in a transaction. I have worked with quite a few real estate agents and Chuck is right at the top of my list of good ones. Actually, Chuck is first and foremost just a good person, and he carries his personal honesty and integrity over into his profession. He has the greatest depth of experience in real estate of any agent or broker I have known. His years of practicing real estate law prior to becoming a broker are evident in the meticulous care he takes with the process and documentation. I am impressed by the way Chuck has integrated internet services into his real estate business. He probably knows more about this process than any other Realtor in the country. In this tight market it is important to use every possible means to spread the word about available properties…to reach the few people who might be interested in a particular property. Steve L.

A Deep Passion. We moved to the Sequim area from Northern New Jersey, just outside of New York City. We didn't know anyone in the area and searched the Internet for a Realtor. Chuck Marunde had an excellent internet presence and deep passion for the Sequim area. We emailed our home specifications and ended up buying the first house he showed us! Chuck responded to every request and was with us through all the closing procedures. He always made us feel like we were his only client. You can't have a better Realtor than Chuck Marunde! Dennis W.

Never Felt Pressured. Working with Chuck Marunde has indeed been a pleasure. Joan and I have been impressed by his quick understanding of what we were looking for and his ability to quickly identify candidate properties which met our criteria. This was especially important to us, as we were relocating from northern Virginia; the time, distance and expense made it desirable for us to make only a few trips to Washington. His patience and insights were extremely valuable in helping us evaluate homes we examined together. We never felt rushed or pressured and always felt that we were in good hands. Chuck's understanding of the Sequim and Port Angeles real estate market enabled us to find an ideal home at a price we are happy with. If you are looking for real estate in the Sequim/Port Angeles area, we highly recommend Chuck as "the go to guy". Arthur R., Lovettsville, VA

Low Key. Working with Chuck while we house-hunted in Sequim was a pleasure. He was very low-key and friendly, and his local knowledge helped us immensely. I especially appreciated his honesty; he wasn't afraid to point out problems with various properties and whether they were overpriced—or, in the case of the home we ultimately bought—underpriced. There was never a hint of hard-sell, just good old-fashioned service. I'd recommend Chuck for any prospective Sequim homebuyer. Doug L.

Site is All Encompassing. We do our homework for the task at hand and we look for and expect to enlist partners that do the same. It was our good fortune to select Chuck Marunde of *Sequim and Port Angeles Real Estate* (dba *iRealty Virtual Brokers*) to represent us as a buyer's broker in our search for a home in the Sequim/Port Angeles area. Chuck's site is all encompassing and super fast compared to many others. He knows the market at every conceivable level, and his guidance through the process of selecting and purchasing a home is priceless - above and beyond that of anyone with whom we have ever worked. Add to all this his 20 year background in real estate law and you have discovered a superb asset in the adventure of purchasing a home. Greg and Marilyn

Unfamiliar With The Area. As an out of state buyer unfamiliar with the area, it was important to me not only to have a real estate agent who knew the area well, but also one who knew the value of the properties. I chose Chuck because he is also a real estate lawyer and it is reassuring to have that extra degree working for you. I selected the houses I was interested in online before taking a two day trip to Sequim to look at them in person. I sent my list to Chuck, who gave me feedback, then organized our tour so we could see 16 properties in a short time. He was very accommodating, driving me all over Sequim, and rescheduling appointments when we fell behind on our time. On day two, I found my home and we drafted an offer on it that evening. By the time I arrived back home on the plane the next evening, my offer had been accepted. Chuck was honest about what it would take to get me into my new home, while having my back the entire transaction. Since I was unable to relocate immediately after closing, he and his assistant, have been taking care of many additional responsibilities for me. He was a pleasure to work with. Chris D.

A Short Escrow. The best decision I made, once I settled on Sequim as the ideal place to spend the rest of my days, was to hook up with Chuck Marunde as my broker/go-to guy. He happily took on the entire complicated merry-go-round associated with a long distance move that involved selling in Southern California (with a different agent) and buying in Sequim – all in the span of just over a month. The unexpectedly quick sale of my previous home was already a week into a 30 day escrow when I got to Sequim for my house hunt. We had two days to find my slice of heaven. And day one was less than stellar, each home having at least one major issue. The killer was the dream home that turned out to be an unmitigated disaster once we got inside. I was crushed. Chuck had his work cut out for him that night. And he worked his magic. On day two there was one beautiful possibility, but not quite right. Suffice to say, in the early afternoon we pulled into a driveway and the first words out of my mouth were "That's my house." 29 days later I took possession of my new home. Every sale has its issues, but throwing in the complications of a short escrow on top of 1200 miles of separation from all documentation, etc. gives new meaning to "challenging". Thanks to his encyclopedic knowledge coupled with a great sense of humor, Chuck was able to keep me on an even keel when things got dicey. He knows when to step in and when to let it evolve. I cannot imagine making this move without him. Rebecca B.

From Port Angeles to Port Townsend. During

the months of February and March 2012, Chuck showed my wife and I over two dozen homes from Port Angeles to Port Townsend. We found Chuck to be very helpful, friendly and courteous. With Chuck there is no pressure; It is all about finding the best home for the buyer. As a Buyer's Agent, Chuck will give you his honest opinion of a property, including a fair market price. In one instance Chuck wrote up an offer for us which was accepted. Chuck was very helpful arranging for home and well inspections which involved multiple trips to the property. Unfortunately, escrow failed to close when, during the home inspection process, it was determined that a septic system repair was needed which the seller was unwilling/unable to make. And we did find our dream home and bought it with Chuck's help, and what a water view we have. We love our home. We feel there is no better Buyer's Agent on the North Olympic. Bert and Sally

Dream Home Became Reality Over a year ago, during a visit to the Olympic Game Farm, we developed what we eventually called the "Sequim Syndrome." We live in New Mexico and decided Sequim was where we wanted to live in retirement. On our second visit to Sequim, we met with Chuck and asked him to help us. Chuck's web site provides such amazing search capabilities. Chuck's site also contains

1,700 blog postings and a real estate video series detailing buying real estate in Sequim. We bought Chuck's book about Sequim real estate and set out to follow his advice carrying on an ongoing email and phone conversation with Chuck. Doing our due diligence "Marunde style" and using his MLS search site, we came up with about 50 homes that met our needs. We narrowed the list down to 15 properties that best met our needs. We came back to Sequim a third time with our list in hand, and Chuck spent two days with us showing us all the homes on our list. Not only did Chuck help us find that dream home, he spent time to educate us about the quality of construction, fair market values of various properties, home layouts, and the joys of Sequim living. We had a great time as we traveled from house to house. By mid afternoon of the second day, my wife said we had found "the house." Chuck helped us draft our offer and sent our offer to the seller's agent. It turned out there was a second offer made on the property at the same time. Chuck's help to make a clean offer paid off. At breakfast two days later, we got a call from Chuck saying our offer had been accepted by the sellers. While we were back in New Mexico Chuck attended every inspection on our behalf, updating us at every turn by email and phone. Our dream home became a reality because of Chuck and because we were smart enough to follow his advice. We absolutely would NOT have been able to do this without Chuck Marunde's expertise and enthusiasm. We recommend Chuck to everyone planning a move to Sequim, Port Angeles, or anywhere on the Olympic Peninsula. Chuck is a gold mine of information and expertise for home buyers everywhere. Larry and Shirley

High Bank Waterfront. We are ex-Washington residents who currently live in Arizona. We had been searching the Puget Sound area four years for a waterfront property to build a retirement home when we first contacted Chuck Marunde through his website. We had made multiple trips to various areas but most of the Realtors we contacted simply sent us an email, provided no follow up and did next to nothing to help us locate a property. On our first trip to Port Angeles, after connecting with Chuck, we purchased our dream property. We now own a high bank waterfront lot overlooking the Straight of Jaun de Fuca, and are excited to become part of the Peninsula community. Paul and Linda

The Hollywood Endorsement. Andy Romano is a successful motion picture character actor with over 40 years in "the Biz." Mr. Romano has a home in beautiful Santa Barbara, California, but he chooses to live most of the time in Sequim, Washington on the Olympic Peninsula in the great Pacific Northwest. Why? In his own words, "Because it's even more beautiful and surrounded by more beauty in this incredibly peaceful and quiet place. With respect to real estate agents or brokers, well my friend Chuck Marunde, owner of *Sequim and Port Angeles Real Estate*, is hands down the best there is." Andy R.

Looked in California, Oregon, North Carolina and Vermont. "We contacted Chuck about six months ago to help find a retirement property in Sequim. We had visited Sequim several weeks before and decided that this was the place for us to retire. We liked the friendly people and the natural beauty of the area. We had been looking for some time in other parts of the country - California, Oregon, North Carolina, and Vermont. In most of these other areas, we found real estate agents that were knowledgeable but did not follow up with us to continue narrowing down real estate possibilities. Once we were out of earshot, communications would stop. That is one of the reasons we were interested in working with Chuck. Besides having great knowledge of both the local real estate market and of law, his testimonials on the internet indicated a willingness to actively communicate with his clients. Chuck demonstrated this immediately. Even before we met, he responded very quickly and helpfully to any email question. After arriving for a second visit to Sequim in September, we finally met Chuck face to face. He was friendly, encouraging, and readily shared good practical information. We worked with him on a number of candidate properties - including an offer on a property while visiting that week. Although we could not come to terms with the owners on the final property price, we look forward to continuing to work closely with Chuck. He is an invaluable resource to help us identify and purchase the retirement property that's right for us." Paul and Virginia

From 800 Miles Away. We can't say enough about working with Chuck Marunde. Luck would have it that we discovered his web site, spoke with him on the phone and had an instant feeling that we had found our Realtor. And we were right. With Chuck's help and expertise, our longtime dream to retire to the Pacific Northwest came to fruition with Chuck assisting us in finding the perfect home. Buying a home is always a big decision and these days can be complex with unexpected delays. In fact, our whole experience from offer day to closing, was very smooth. Chuck took all the time we needed to explain processes and made us feel at ease, even though we lived 800 miles away, tying up loose ends and getting ready for the big move to our new home in Sequim. We were impressed with Chuck's ability to listen to our needs and understand our concerns in buying from a distance. Chuck kept us informed all along the way, during the process and was so good at getting right back to us if we had another question. All went so well and Chuck really went above and beyond for us, taking time out from his busy schedule to assist us with some details regarding our beautiful property, even after the closing, because we were not yet arrived there. Without hesitation, our son and his wife will be contacting Chuck this summer, as they plan to follow us to paradise in this lovely town. Thanks again Chuck, for everything! Mary and Jerry

<u>Intending to Interview Several Realtors</u>. My husband and I went to Sequim intending to interview several Realtors to find one to help us locate and buy a home in Sequim. We knew we wanted someone we could trust and who would have our best interests in mind. Since we would be handling the transaction from S. California this was very important to us. We met Chuck and looked no further. We felt a connection right away and spent some time looking at homes together so Chuck could get a feel for what we wanted. Well, we left Sequim having made an offer on a home which the owner accepted. Chuck has helped us through the purchase process. We are positive it would not have gone so smoothly without his help. We give him 4 thumbs up. Wally & Cathy

<u>It Took Two Weeks</u>. My wife and I moved to Sequim six weeks ago, and prior to our move here I

contacted Chuck Marunde and enlisted his help as our buyer's agent. Once we got here, it took us about two weeks looking at houses, and Chuck did a superb job of showing us places and letting us make our own decisions and guide us through the purchase of our home. We now completed our transaction and are very happy. We would recommend Chuck to anybody. Don & Marilyn

Gender Neutrality

The National Association of Realtors once published a report that identified the average American Realtor as a 51 year old woman. Of course, there is no such thing as an average Realtor, but I think the point was that there are more women than men in real estate sales, and the average age of Realtors was about 51.[1] The truth is Realtors in the U.S. are almost evenly divided between men and woman. With that in mind, the pronouns in this book could refer to a man as much as they could a woman.

Gender neutrality in literature is often achieved by inserting both feminine and masculine pronouns every time a third party pronoun is used. Many sentences in this book would have been so full of "him or her" ("him/her"), "he or she" ("he/she"), "his or her's" ("his/her's"), "himself or herself" ("himself/herself"), this approach would have interrupted the readability.

Some writers simply alternate between masculine and feminine pronouns throughout their writings. I think that is the best approach. It seems to make the material easier to read and does not interrupt the flow of thought. This is the approach I've taken in this book, although I randomly used masculine or feminine pronouns, not alternating precisely from one to the other. That worked best for me, because I don't write a book in chronological order from chapter to chapter.

---

[1] National Association of Realtors Member Profile 2012

Online Resources

SequimRealEstateBlog.com
(Larest RE Blog in the County and Peninsula
with over 1,700 Articles)

Sequim-Homes.com
(The Olympic Listing Service, OLS)

SequimForSale.com
(The OLS + Northwest MLS)

SequimRealEstateBooks.com

Sequim-Washington-Homes.com
(Real Estate Q&A Site)

365ThingsToDoInSequim.com

SequimPhotos.com

LuxuryWaterViewHomes.com

Made in the USA
San Bernardino, CA
16 March 2015